PIECES OF HISTORY:
ARTIFACTS OF
THE PT BOAT NAVY

Higgins Hellcat (PT 564)

FRANK J. ANDRUSS SR.

NIMBLE BOOKS LLC

Nimble Books LLC

Nimble Books LLC

2846 S. Knightsbridge Circle

Ann Arbor, MI, USA 48105

http://www.NimbleBooks.com

wfz@nimblebooks.com

Copyright 2020 Frank J. Andruss Sr.

Version 1.0; last saved 2021-02-01.

Printed in the United States of America

ISBN-13: 9781608882038

Front cover: the Higgins Hellcat, better known as PT 564. Seventy feet in length and built in 1943, she was never put into production because the Navy felt she was too small to carry the weapons needed. She could run at 47 or so knots and out-maneuver any other PT. NavSource Online writes that "[…at a Navy Department conference in November 1943] it was decided that various considerations favored continued production of the larger types. Most of the PT actions in the Pacific at that time were against barges—the boats were being used primarily as gunboats and had to carry considerable weight in guns and ammunition in addition to their torpedoes. A big boat was required to carry the load. In many forward areas the crews had to live and eat aboard the boats for weeks at a time. The Hellcat had no galley or refrigerator; its living accommodations were inadequate for that type of operation. A new boat would require retooling. And though it had passed its trials with flying colors, there was a possibility that performance in service would disclose defects not apparent in the trials." (Photo: Naval History and Heritage Command)

CONTENTS (INCLUDING FIGURES)

NIMBLE BOOKS LLC

FOREWORD

Ahoy. I am Arthur John Frongello, Quartermaster Third Class, RON 22, PT 302, and honored to write this Foreword.

The ocean is my passion. As a young boy my mother, Freda, and my aunt Mary would round up all the kids in the neighborhood who had the ten-cent care fare and we would all head for Castle Island, one of the beaches in Boston Harbor. Lunch was homemade pasta and for dinner we dug clams in the mud flats and cooked them on open fires on the beach.

At 18, I left my second year of high school to join the Navy—a decision preempted by the threat of getting drafted into the Army.

Great choice as I was sent to Newport, Rhode Island for boot training. Out of boot camp and still at Newport, I was selected to attend Quartermaster School. A "salute and shoot deal" as I had no choice. When they told me I would be learning navigation I said what a joke, as I get lost on the Boston subway.

Newport was when I saw the PT boats going in and out of Melville. The top ten percent of the class could make that choice I did.

What an experience, what a way to fight a war—from the deck of a very expensive 80-foot yacht! Yes, I got sea-sick, but my ship mates helped me through until I got my sea legs. I discovered a family away from home. Dropping out never entered my mind.

Training ended and I was deployed to Italy and set foot on PT 302. Most of the crew were new so it gave us a chance to learn to work and get along with each other. My skipper was an old man of twenty-nine from New Orleans and he really knew small boats. He helped me and taught me so much. The rest of the crew were like I said, family. Sharing was the rule of the day.

My sea legs would come and go. When on patrol my shipmates would hold me over a torpedo tube as I donated to the sea. After which, we all had a good laugh. I was always happy to return safely from patrol.

War is no school for heroes. We were just young boys growing to be young men. We finished the war in Europe and my RON was returned to New York City to be refurbished for duty in the Pacific. The Big Bomb ended World War II. I became a civilian again and returned to finish high school.

Thanks to dedicated patriots like Frank J. Andruss Sr. our memories are made into history. You have permission to "come aboard" by turning these pages. Enjoy this rendezvous with the past!

Arthur J. Frongello
QM3/c PT 302

PREFACE

During World War Two the US Navy constructed patrol torpedo (PT) boats which, unsurprisingly, carried torpedoes as well as several types of guns. The torpedo capability was singled out for mention in the class designation because a torpedo is a threat to *any* enemy ship, however large. Thus, PT boats, despite their small size, were full-fledged members of the battle force.

The PT boats quickly found their way to the war front and proved their worth. Over the years these wooden boats and the men that served on them would attack many types of targets, including enemy shipping, large capital ships, enemy shore installations, and supply barges. The crews of the little boats brought the fight to the enemy using their skill and daring, often at night, on seemingly endless patrols.

Every man who served on a PT boat had a story to tell of those dark days of the war. They lived and died on these boats and many of them brought home items and artifacts they had collected over the years. In some small way bringing home a treasured artifact of their time spent on the boats kept their memories alive.

My passion for the history of the PT boats began as a very young child, when, in 1967, my Dad suggested that I watch the movie *PT 109*. This started my life-long journey in which as a young twenty-year-old I had the pleasure of meeting so many PT boat veterans and started to collect some of these treasured artifacts of the PT Navy. Over the years I would begin to create "The Mosquito Fleet Exhibit" in which I would use these artifacts to tell the story and provide the history that so many people did not know about.

I got the idea for this book after doing two other books, *Building the PT Boats* (Nimble Books, 2010; ISBN 978-1608880737) and *PT Boats Behind the Scenes* (Nimble Books, 2011; ISBN 978-1608881499*)*. Over the past few years many authors have come forward with new books about the boats and pretty much all of the subject matter has been done. I did not want to do anything that would require a rehashing of this familiar material, so I thought it was time for something new— but what? Surrounded as I am each day by artifacts that had been donated, it only made sense to tell their story using photos and descriptions of these artifacts. History at its finest.

In doing this book one of the hardest things was trying to include artifacts that would be most interesting to the reader. For me it is all important and is a large part of each person's story. In this book you will find artifacts not only from the sailors but from three of the builders of these wonderful boats. The Elco Naval Division did an excellent job of keeping their boats in the public eye, and for that reason you will see mostly artifacts from them and those that worked within their company. During the war years the PT boats were the darlings of the Navy and much was written about them, especially when the US needed victories in the early days of the war. There was just something special about the David and Goliath myth that so encompassed the little boats and the men that fought in them.

It is my hope that, through these artifacts that were such a large part of PT history, this book brings new attention to the PT navy during World War II. In this book I hope to tell the stories of the brave sailors that served on the boats. PT boats played important roles from the first days of the war. They were in the Philippines, at Guadalcanal, at New Guinea, in the Med, at Surigao Strait. Their crews deserve to be remembered when World War II history is told. Although the PT boat has long since gone, the bravery of the men who rode on her decks should never be forgotten.

ACKNOWLEDGMENTS

I have so many people to thank in assisting me throughout the making of this book. First and foremost, I must thank my wife Stacia who has put up with my love for the history of the PT boats for the past 42 years. She is my soul mate and without her I would be lost.

Second, I give special thanks to those that served on our World War Two PT boats, bases, and tenders. They were the "Greatest Generation" and helped pave the way to victory. I have had the honor to meet so many of them over the years from across the country and have found them to be a special class of officers and sailors. They have always taken me in and treated me like family. Most have taken their final patrol, but some are still here with us, well into their nineties, still ready to ride the boats if they could.

Special thanks to my grandsons Dominick, Frankie, and Charlie who although are still young might someday get bitten by the PT bug like I did some 45 years ago. It is my hope and dream that they will enjoy the history and take the time to learn about these special men and the work they did during World War Two.

I owe a debt of gratitude to Wally Boerger from Save the PT Boat Inc, for his assistance in providing me with many photos to choose for the book. Thanks to Alyce Guthrie from PT BOATS, Inc. who always provides sound advice and has been a joy to talk with over the many years I have known her. Special thanks to my dear friend Arthur Frongello who at 96 years of age can still man his station on PT 302 as Quartermaster. His friendship has meant a great deal over the years. Thanks so much to Jon Olson from YKO Studio LLC for helping me fix many of the photos and to James Sawyer for doing the same. Thanks to Charlie B. Jones and Andrew Small for being there when I needed them.

I am indebted to the PT boat veterans who have donated so many artifacts to me. I shall never forget you.

Special thanks to all of you that have believed in the work I have been doing for so many years in trying to keep the PT boat service in the public eye. It has been plenty of hard work, but the rewards have been wonderful.

NIMBLE BOOKS LLC

INTRODUCTION

In the early days before World War Two the United States did not give any real thought to motor torpedo boats (MTBs). During the interwar years, countries such as Britain and Italy were making far reaching strides in this type design and improving their tactics. Somehow a boat that could maneuver in shallow waters, fire torpedoes and was of small design never really attracted attention in the US. The Navy General Board was hesitant to experiment with these small offensive boats and felt it was not a good time for these type craft to be built in any large numbers.

As the US Navy kept tabs on other countries, it began to see that it could no longer ignore the fact that these boats could have some usefulness, for example in attacking enemy shipping. In 1920 the Secretary of the Navy approved a recommendation to purchase two Thornycroft Royal Navy Coastal Motor Boats (CMBs). One was a 40-foot craft while the other of the 55-foot class. It did however take two years before the Navy began running tests on these boats which could make 32 and 35 knots respectively. Not much was done to follow up, but the US began to take notice when Hubert Scott-Paine designed a 60-foot British MTB in 1934. In 1937 the Secretary of the Navy sent a letter to the General Board requesting that that they should make a complete study of the MTBs and submit a report with opinions on the value of the type to the Navy.

Paine designed a boat in 1939 which would have far reaching effects on the US Navy and its PT program. His boat was greeted with much enthusiasm both by the yachting community and by the Navy powers that be. His new design was 70 feet overall and would carry two 21-inch torpedoes or four 18-inch torpedoes. She would be lightly armored, having two 20-mm and one 25-mm cannon which were mounted in power turrets. For the first time a MTB would be constructed of largely wood, which saved weight with no loss of strength.

When the United States finally began building of these small boats, much testing had already been done. The Electric Boat Company (or Elco) in Bayonne, New Jersey, had secured one of the Scott-Paine boats, while other companies such as Higgins Industries in New Orleans and Huckins Yacht Works in Florida built their own using the specs from the design contest. Competition trials would result those companies being awarded contracts to build the US Navy PT boats.

Development over the years leading up to World War Two was not without its problems, but the boat building companies were constantly doing what they could to produce better boats with better capabilities. The weapons they built enabled the American PT navy during World War Two to performed with honor and courage in the face of the enemy. All who served did so in keeping with the highest traditions of the US Navy.

ARTIFACTS FROM THE BUILDERS

The three main builders for the American PT boats were the Elco Naval Division located in Bayonne, New Jersey; Higgins Industries located in New Orleans; and the Huckins Yacht Corporation in Florida.

There is no doubt that Elco was the front-runner when it came to keeping their PT boats in the public eye. They believed in a photographic campaign second to none, and hired well-known photographic illustrator Morris Rosenfeld of New York to do much of their work. Elco created many artifacts pertaining to the PT boats (today, they would be called "marketing collateral" or "swag"). Elco even had an employee, Don Rosencrantz, who worked in the hull department, building metal and wood factory models. They had many giveaways for dignitaries that visited the plant.

In this section you will see that the majority of the following photos deal with Elco. Higgins and Huckins artifacts are most difficult to locate and it is apparent that these builders did not have the publicity campaign in mind that Elco did. What you will view here for Higgins Industries and Huckins Yacht is a very tiny piece of their past because these artifacts just do not exist, or they are in collections not known to the public.

Figure 1. RON 28 decal that I took off of the tool room wall when I visited Elco in 1998. It remains one of my prized possessions. Equipped only with a ladder, a hammer, a screw driver and a hack saw blade with no handle, I got it! I cut my hand in the process and bled on my friend below who was holding the ladder for me. I was determined not to leave Elco without this wonderful piece. Six decals were on the wall, but a broken window that was letting in the elements had destroyed the first five in that row, the sixth being this one. (Frank J. Andruss Sr. collection)

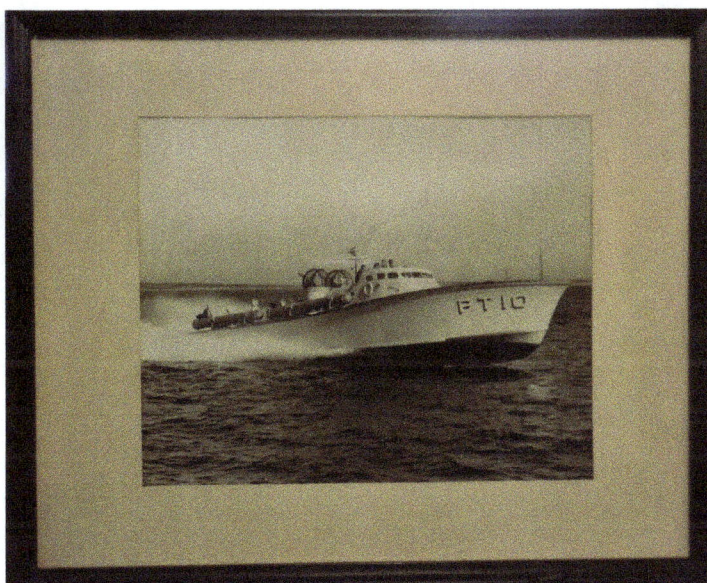

Figure 2. Framed picture of PT 10. This was Elco's first assembled seventy-foot boat. This picture was removed from the main offices of Building 20 by Elco employee Charles Waller. (Frank J. Andruss Sr. collection)

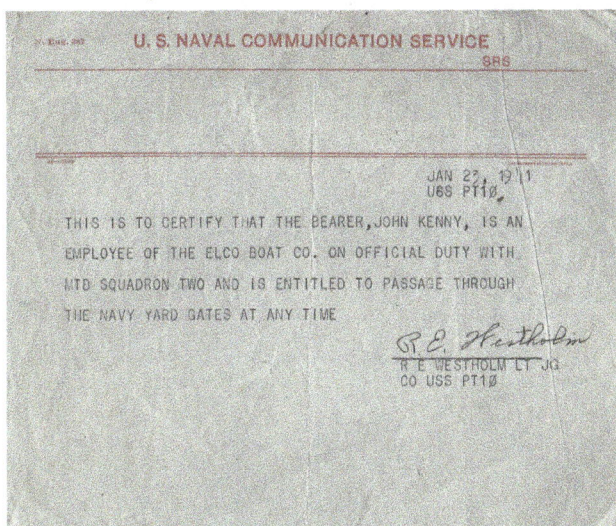

Figure 3. Rare gate pass for Elco employee and electrical engineer John C. Kenny. Kenny was on official duty with MTB Squadron 2 and would later ride with the seventy-foot Elco boats from Florida to Cuba for their shakedown cruise. The gate pass is signed by the CO of PT 10, Lt. R.E. Westholm. (Frank J. Andruss Sr. collection)

Figure 4. Elco ID Badges. The blue ID Badge was given to those first time workers that were learning the job in different departments, while the EXHT ID was for the engine shop. (Frank J. Andruss Sr. collection)

Figure 5. Rare Elco presentation box showing PT 10 on the cover. Not many of these were produced and they were only handed out to a select group of Elco employees. They were small enough to carry matchbooks or business cards. This box belonged to Elco employee Glenville Tremaine who was the Works Manager in the main office.(Frank J. Andruss Sr. collection)

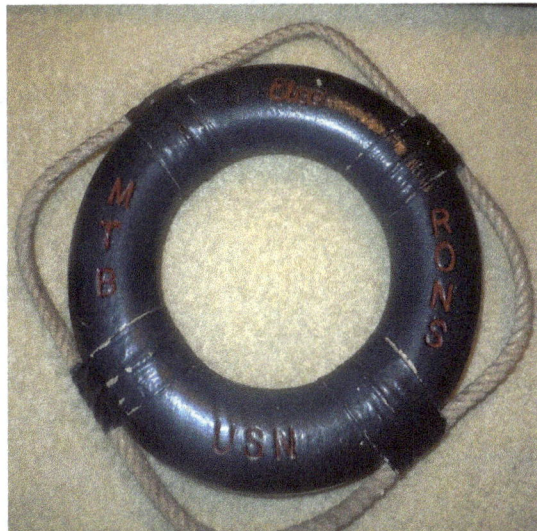

Figure 6. Elco Life Ring decorative piece showing the Elco RONs. This was in the office of Managing Constructor Irwin Chase while working at Elco. (Frank J. Andruss Sr. collection)

Figure 7. Original Elco Shop jacket. All of the workers wore white with blue trim usually coveralls while working at the plant. This shop jacket was part of the Elco Sheet Metal Department and belonged to Foreman E. F. Garrigan. (Frank J. Andruss Sr. collection)

Figure 8. Photo of Elco's Sheet Metal Department. Mr. Garrigan is far right first row with a clean shop jacket on, no doubt for the photo. (Frank J. Andruss Sr. collection)

Figure 9. Elco's first assembled 103-class eighty-foot boat. The ceremonies were for Saturday, May 16th 1942 with the sponsor being Mrs. John D. Bulkeley, wife of the Medal of Honor-winning PT captain. The photo from F. W. Rowe, assistant Supervisor of Ships at Elco, shows the 103 boat while in the boat basin at Eco on this day. (Frank J. Andruss Sr. collection)

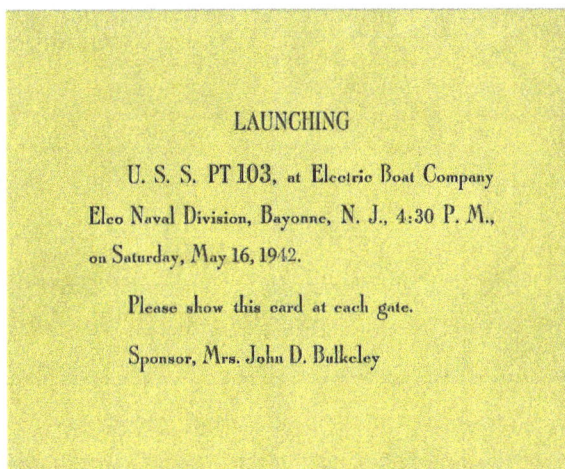

LAUNCHING

U. S. S. PT 103, at Electric Boat Company
Elco Naval Division, Bayonne, N. J., 4:30 P. M.,
on Saturday, May 16, 1942.

Please show this card at each gate.

Sponsor, Mrs. John D. Bulkeley

Figure 10. Original gate pass from Elco for the launching of PT 103. (Frank J. Andruss Sr. collection)

Figure 11. A framed print of Elco's PT 117 removed from the office of General Manager Preston L. Sutphen after the war by Elco office worker Charles Waller. (Frank J. Andruss Sr. collection)

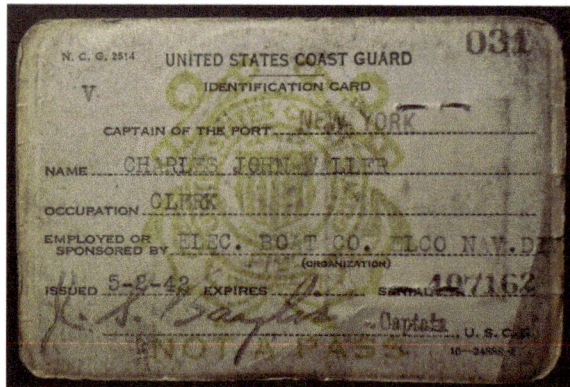

Figure 12. Another type of ID badge at Elco was cardboard or plastic covered. This first ID belonged to Charles John Waller who worked in Building 21 as a clerk. He would later be responsible for the liquidation of items before the plant would close in 1949. Waller was an exceptional athlete and played on Elco's Industrial league Soccer, Softball, and Bowling teams. (Frank J. Andruss Sr. collection)

Figure 13. This ID belonged to Donald Rosencrantz who would work in the Hull department. It was discovered that Rosencrantz was an exceptional model builder, and when not doing his duties in the Hull department he was drafted to build models for the Company. During his time at Elco it is not known just how many different models he constructed but some of those models can be seen on the following pages. (Frank J. Andruss Sr. collection)

Figure 14. Model of PT 41 made by Rosencrantz and being inspected by Lt. Comdr. John D. Bulkeley and his father Frederick. Rosencrantz is in the crowd with a pipe in his mouth. (Frank J. Andruss Sr. collection)

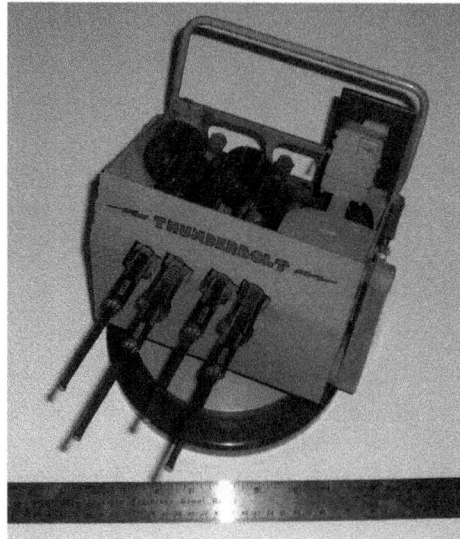

Figure 15 (a) This is the Elco Thunderbolt model that was designed by Elco and made as a presentation model by Don Rosencrantz. This photo showing a metal ruler gives an idea on the size of the model which was constructed mostly of metal parts. (Ed Behney collection)

(b) Side view of the Thunderbolt model showing the 20-mm guns. (Ed Behney collection)

(c) Top view of the Thunderbolt model showing the close quarters of the gunners seat and the guns with ammo canisters. (Ed Behney collection)

Figure 16. Elco matchbook covers showing the PT boats on the cover and the claim as the "world's fastest combat vessel." (Frank J. Andruss Sr. collection)

Figure 17. Elco Matchbooks inside cover: "The Last Word in Pleasure Craft by the First Name in PTs" with the Knights of the Sea logo.

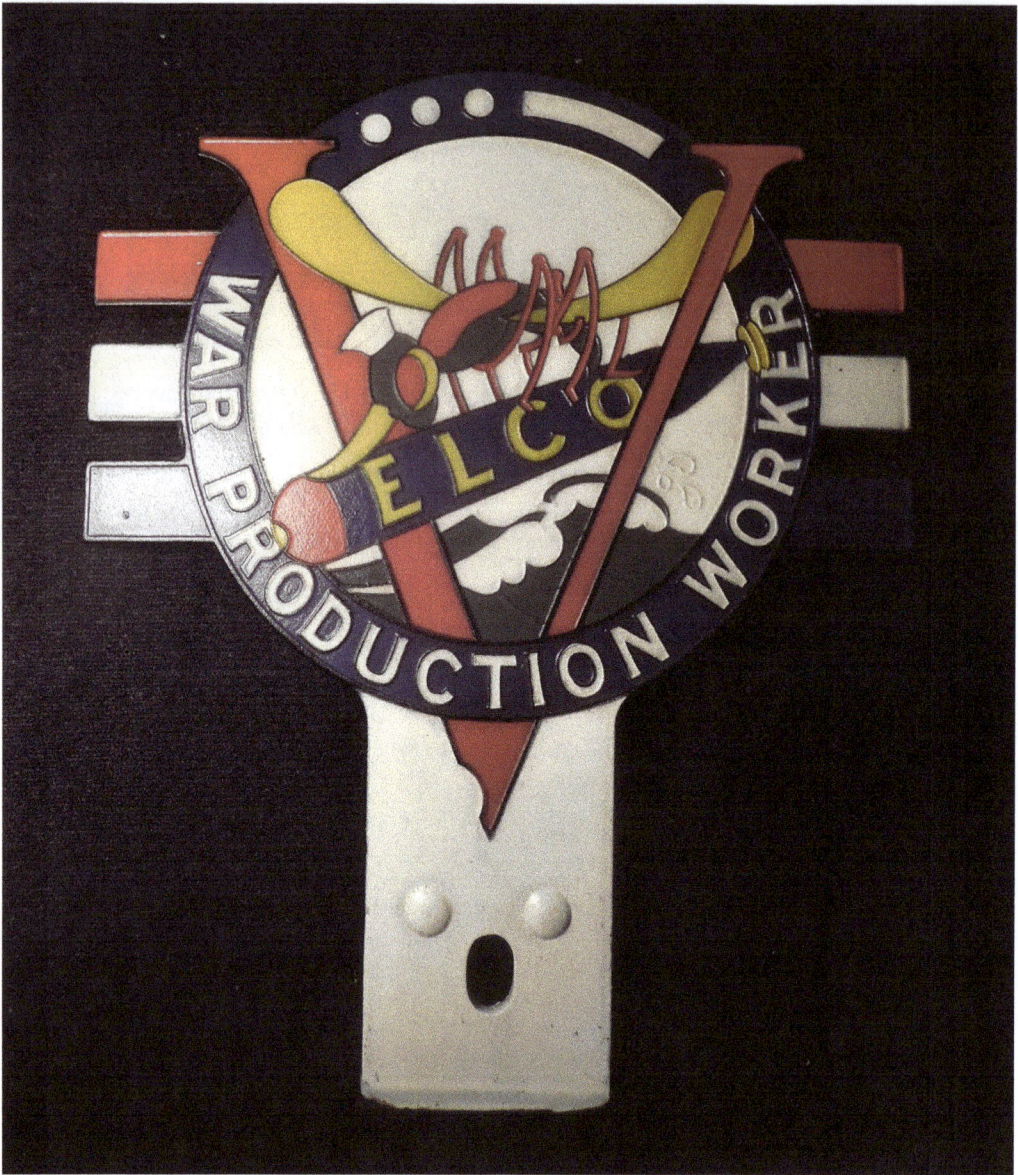

Figure 18. A rare Elco license plate topper made by the company and usually reserved for upper management. This unused topper was made from a Bakelite type of material and belonged to Works Manager Glenville Tremaine. (Frank J. Andruss Sr. collection)

Figure 19. Hand-made jewelry box made from scrap mahogany wood. Many woodworkers and carpenters at Elco made items like this in their spare time for loved ones. This one was made by R.T. Jones. (Frank J. Andruss Sr. collection)

Figure 20. Another angle showing the beauty of the mahogany wood used to make this piece—and the PT boats. Some beautiful photographs of the mahogany construction are found in *Building the PT Boats* (Nimble, 2011). (Frank J. Andruss Sr. collection)

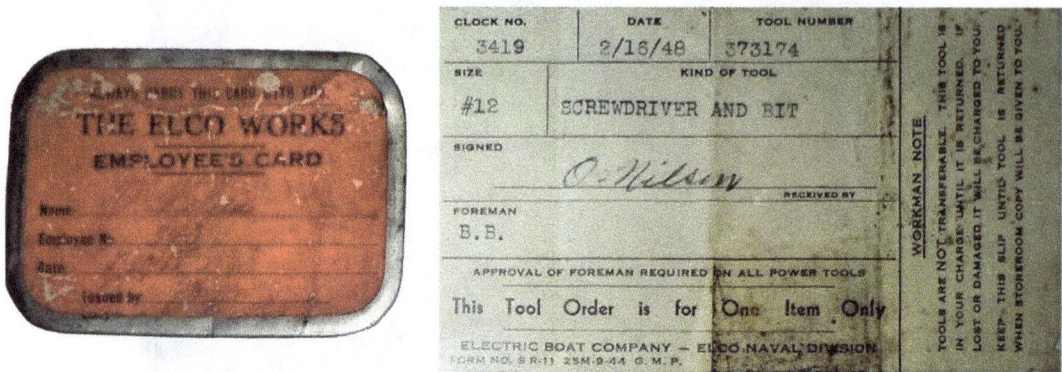

Figure 21. Olav Nilson's Elco ID card and tool slip. Olav was a Scandinavian who joined what was then the Elco Works in 1900. His job was working on the keel of the PT boats using a hand adz. A boat builder by trade, he came to America and worked with Elco until it closed in 1949. (Frank J. Andruss Sr. collection)

Figure 22. Tool box owned by Olav Nilson, which includes his tools, a drill, his thermos bottle, and tin lunch box. (Frank J. Andruss Sr. collection)

Figure 23. Rare pen and ink drawing by Elco employee Malcolm Mchintyre. It is believed that he did at least four others while working at Elco. (Frank J. Andruss Sr. collection)

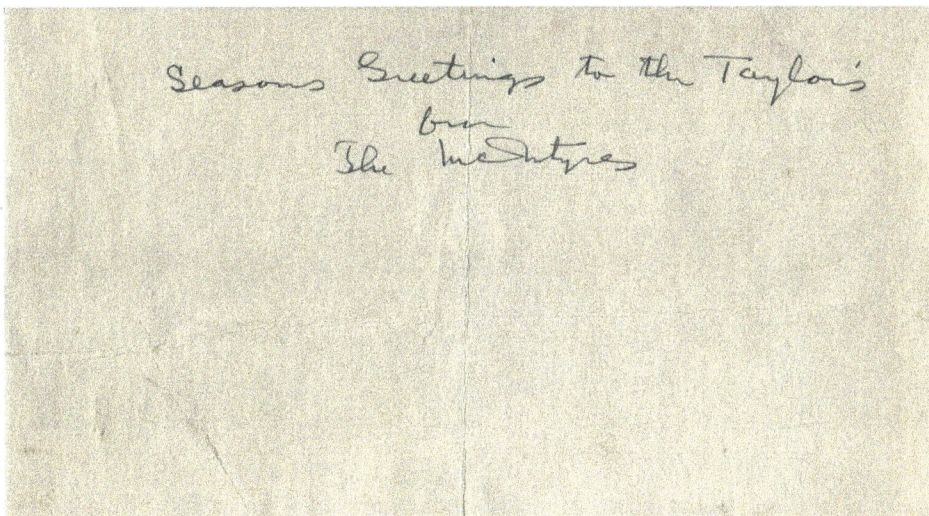

Figure 24. The pen and ink drawing, as rare as it is, becomes even more so as this was sent to the Taylors and signed by the Mchintyre family. (Frank J. Andruss Sr. collection)

Figure 25. Photo of Managing Constructor Irwin Chase. A University of Michigan graduate in Naval Architecture studies, he was hired by Executive Vice President of Elco Henry R. Sutphen in 1906. Chase loved to experiment with high powered-boats and was credited by Elco for designing the world's first planing hull, a twenty-foot Elcoplane named "The Bug" in 1911. Considered the father of the Elco PT boat program he remained with the company until its closing in 1949. (Frank J. Andruss Sr. collection)

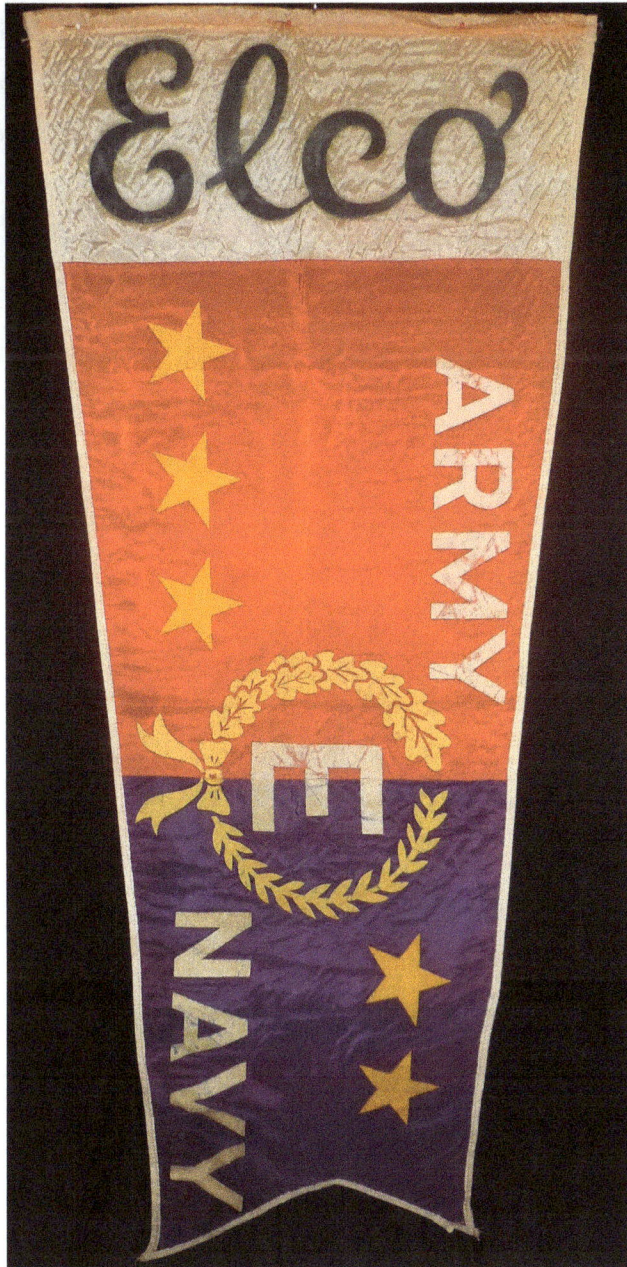

Figure 26. A wonderful and rare example of the Elco Army/Navy E Pennant. This was Elco's fifth award for excellence in productivity. This pennant hung in the office of Irwin Chase. (Frank J. Andruss Sr. collection)

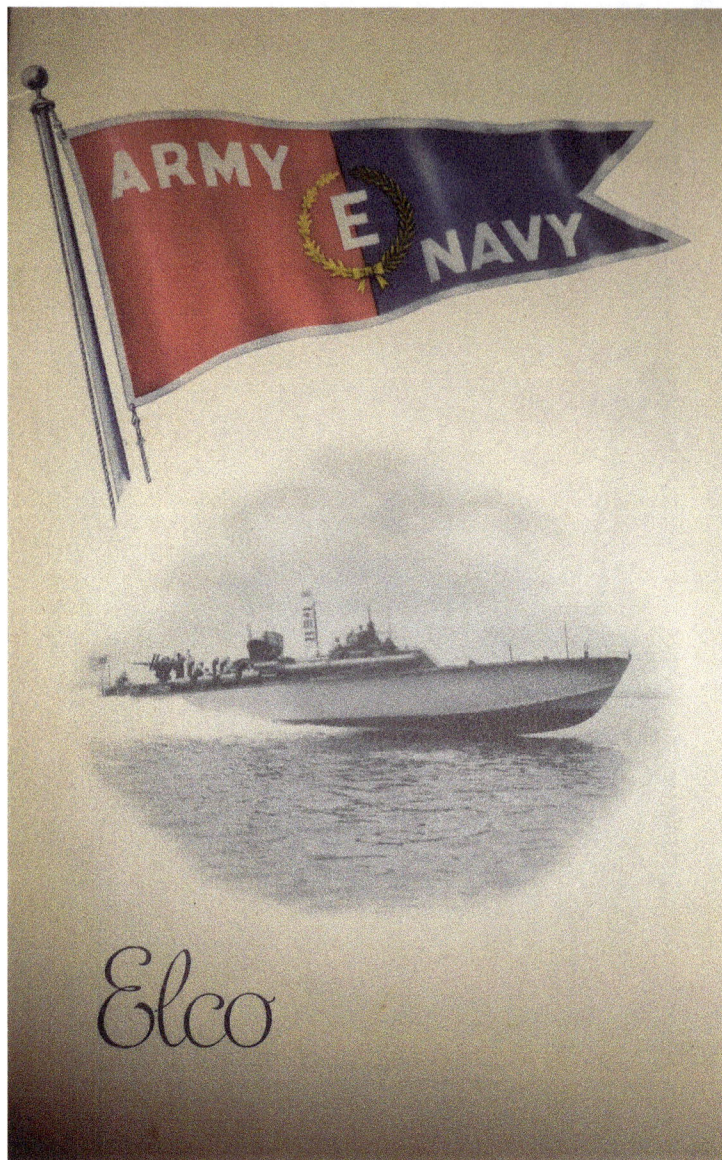

Figure 27. Rare Elco Army/Navy E award booklet that belonged to Irwin Chase. The book is dated 1942 and was in line with the launching of PT 131. An address to the workers included an acceptance speech by Executive Vice President Henry R. Sutphen and remarks by Lt. Cmdr. John D. Bulkeley of RON 3. (Frank J. Andruss Sr. collection)

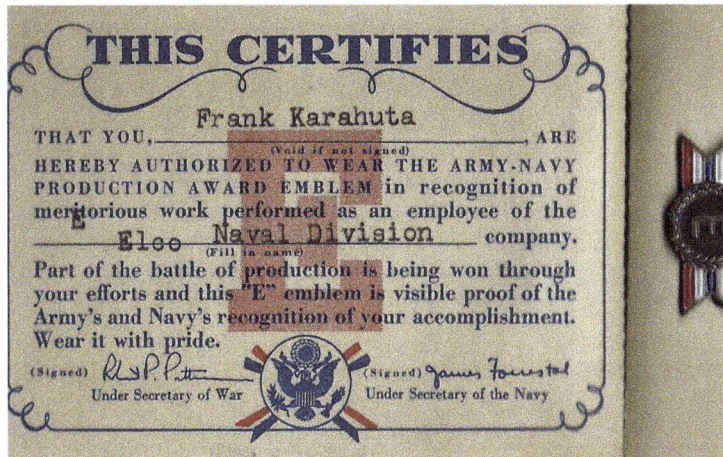

Figure 28. Army/Navy E award presented to Frank Karahuta who worked at the plant. Employees were awarded these cardboard awards each time Elco was presented the award for excellence. (Frank J. Andruss Sr. collection)

Figure 29. Elco Award for Production ideas. This one was awarded to C. Natoli for his idea that contributed to war production within the company. It is signed by Works Manager Glenville Tremaine. (Frank J. Andruss Sr. collection)

Figure 30. The brain trust of the Elco Naval Division. From left: Designer Alfred Fleming, Managing Constructor Irwin Chase, Executive Vice President Henry R. Sutphen, Works Manager Glenville Tremaine, and General Manager Preston L. Sutphen. Notice the wonderful Elco Factory model on the desk. Taken in early 1945.

Figure 31. Pristine example of an original Elco Factory model. Made from metal and wood, these models were farmed out to companies like Comet and Authenticast. They were fine examples of the types of PT boats that Elco was producing for the war effort. This handsome model was a late-war Elco complete with rocket launchers and late-war style radar along with heavy-hitting guns. (Frank J. Andruss Sr. collection)

Figure 32. Photo of the famous Dewitt Theatre in Bayonne, New Jersey. The Warner brothers film *Devil Boats* was shot at the Elco Naval Division and was shown here on August 22, 1944. Elco took over the theatre with over 2800 Elco employees and invited guests that night. Before the showing of the movie Elco was awarded the Army/Navy E Flag for excellence in productivity. (Frank J. Andruss Sr.collection)

Figure 33. Elco brochure and unused ticket for *Devil Boats*. The brochure was handed out to all those that attended the movie and ceremony. (Frank J. Andruss Sr. collection)

Figure 34. Elco office employee Charles J. Waller takes some time off after a long day. Waller was an exceptional athlete even before he worked at Elco and was proficient in soccer, baseball, and bowling. He helped Elco to win several championships in the Industrial Leagues around the New Jersey area.

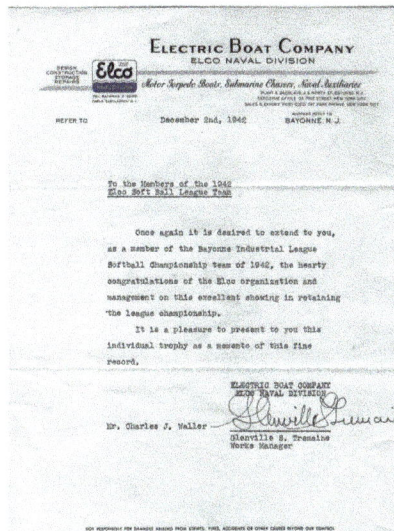

Figure 35. Letter signed by Works Manager Glenville Tremaine sending Elco's congratulations for the softball team winning the Bayonne Industrial League Championship in 1942. The letter was for Waller who led the team in batting that year. (Frank J. Andruss Sr. collection)

Figure 36. Original softball trophy for Charles Waller presented by Elco in 1942. (Frank J. Andruss Sr. collection)

Figure 37. Original Elco sweater and champion softball patch presented to Charles Waller by the Elco Naval Division for again winning the championship in 1944. (Frank J. Andruss Sr. collection)

Figure 38. Photo of one of the Elco-sponsored Christmas dances.

Figure 39. This was an Elco handout signed by many of the employees and office staff. It was given out to those that attended the Christmas dance in the above photo. This one belonged to Elco employee Carolyn Young. (Frank J. Andruss Sr. collection)

Figure 40. First Elco publication: "Elco: the Inside story of Motor Torpedo Boats" This was published in 1942. (Frank J. Andruss Sr. collection)

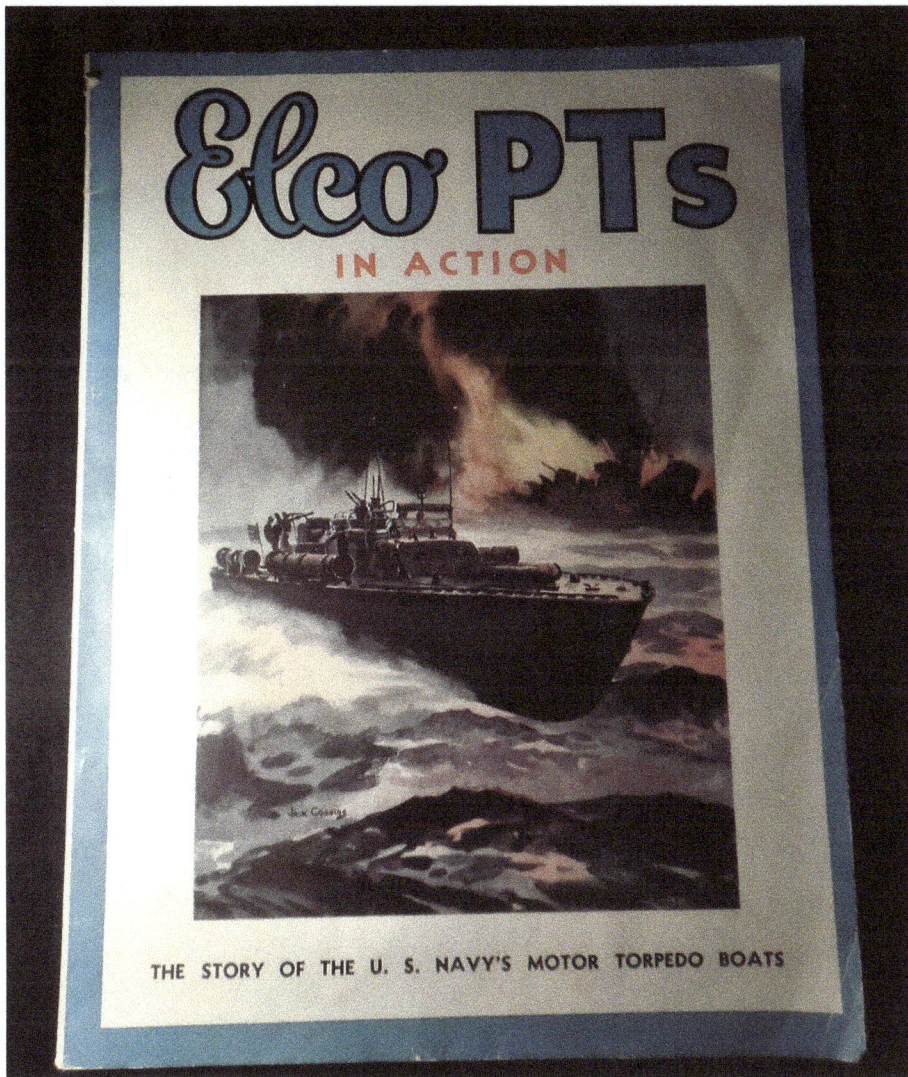

Figure 41. A second Elco publication, "Elco PTs in Action: The Story of the US Navy's Motor Torpedo Boats." This was published in mid-1944. (Frank J. Andruss Sr. collection)

Figure 42. Christmas Card from 1942, this one showing the "Knights of the Sea" print. (Frank J. Andruss Sr. collection)

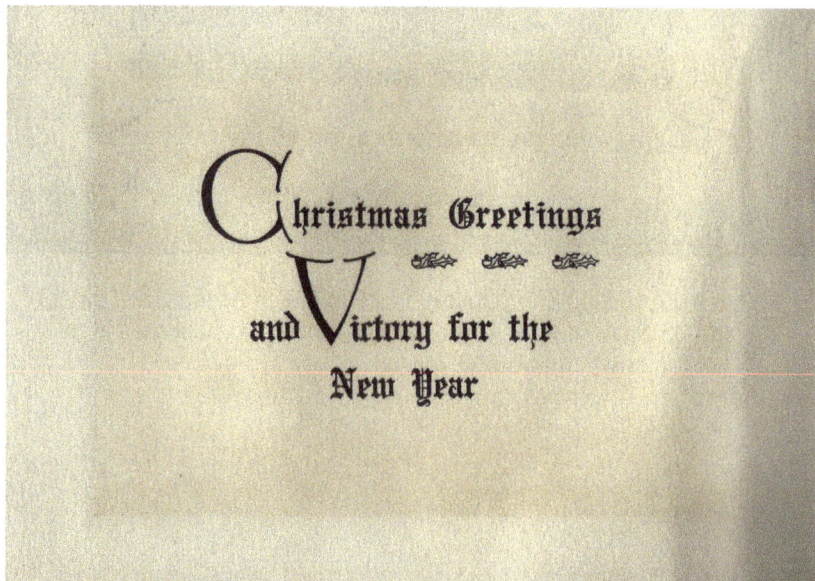

Figure 43. Inside: "Christmas Greetings and Victory for the New Year.". (Frank J. Andruss Sr. collection)

Figure 44. Another type of Christmas card from 1942, showing Elco's beautiful 103-class PT, a color version of PT 117 as she heads through the water. (Frank J. Andruss Sr. collection)

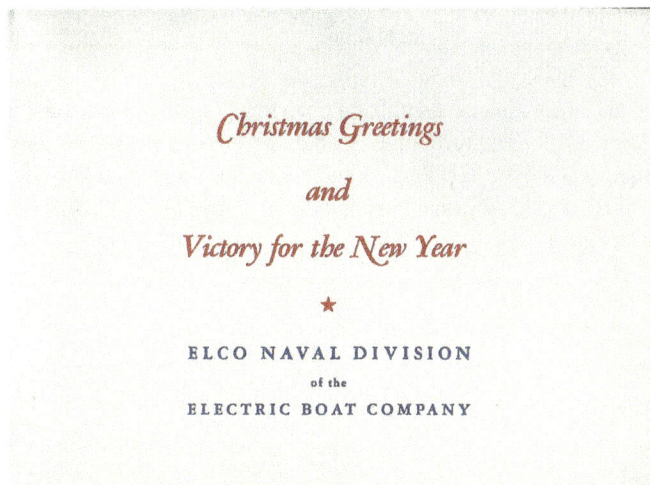

Christmas Greetings

and

Victory for the New Year

★

ELCO NAVAL DIVISION
of the
ELECTRIC BOAT COMPANY

Figure 45. Inside, again with a Christmas greeting and a Victory wish, this time stamped with the company name.. (Frank J. Andruss Sr. collection)

Figure 46. Interesting concept for a Christmas Card. We see the little PT boats emerging from their cradles at Elco to do battle with the enemy against a setting sun and swastika. This was a large card at 8 x 10 and was drawn using pen and ink. (Frank J. Andruss Sr. collection)

Figure 47. Photo of *PT 9*, the Scott-Paine designed seventy-foot boat in which Elco used as a template for their first assembled boats PT 10 through 19. The Walt Disney-designed Mosquito Fleet emblem is on the starboard side forward cabin and was used on the early seventy-foot boats and some of the seventy-seven foot boats as well before being removed.

Figure 48. A fine example of the Mosquito Fleet emblem which was located at the Elco Naval Division offices and removed by office employee Charles Waller. The beauty of this design and color can really be appreciated. (Frank J. Andruss Sr. collection)

Figure 49. Photo of Works Manager Glenville S. Tremaine. Tremaine joined the Electric Launch Company (Elco) of Bayonne, NJ in 1912 as a draftsman. As a naval architect he also designed motor yachts for several well-known people. He became Chief Designer of Elco in 1923 and Works Manager from 1939 until it was closed in 1949. Later he would open up Tremaine Yacht Company in NJ.

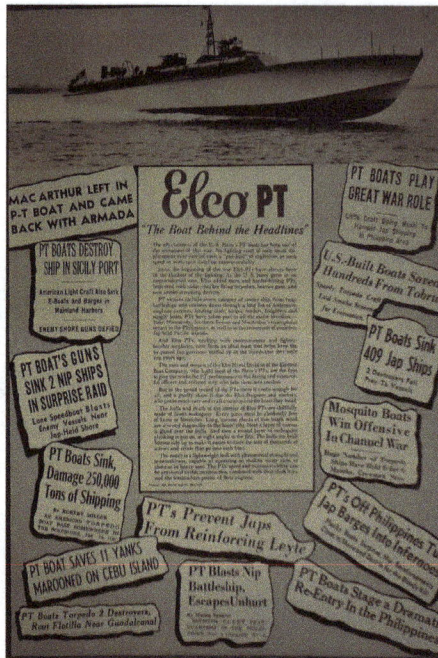

Figure 50. Elco publication and handout for visitors to the plant. Called "The Boat Behind the Headlines" it contained clippings of many of the articles written about the Elco PT boats. This pristine example belonged to Works Manager Glenville Tremaine. (Frank J. Andruss Sr. collection)

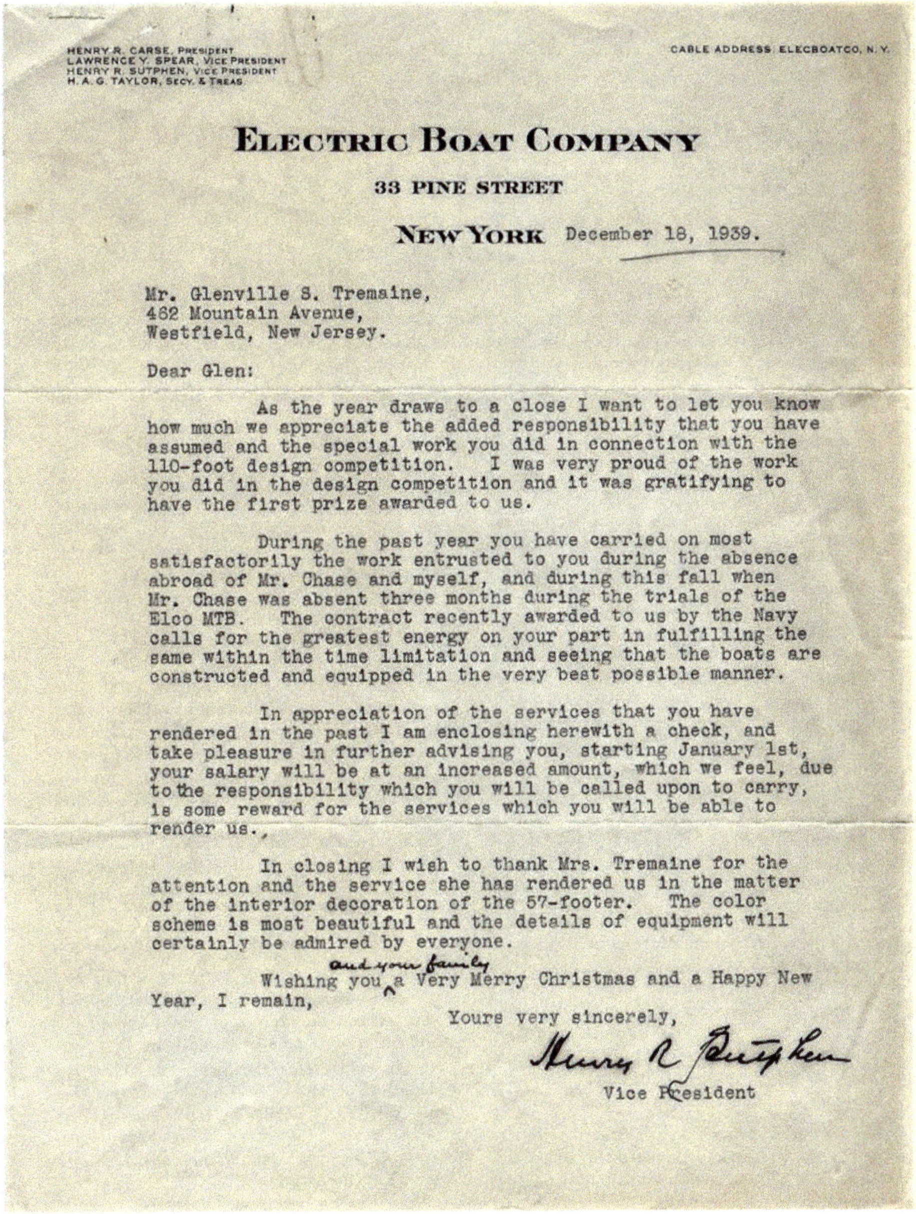

HENRY R. CARSE, PRESIDENT
LAWRENCE Y. SPEAR, VICE PRESIDENT
HENRY R. SUTPHEN, VICE PRESIDENT
H. A. G. TAYLOR, SECY. & TREAS.

CABLE ADDRESS: ELECBOATCO, N.Y.

ELECTRIC BOAT COMPANY

33 PINE STREET

NEW YORK December 18, 1939.

Mr. Glenville S. Tremaine,
482 Mountain Avenue,
Westfield, New Jersey.

Dear Glen:

As the year draws to a close I want to let you know
how much we appreciate the added responsibility that you have
assumed and the special work you did in connection with the
110-foot design competition. I was very proud of the work
you did in the design competition and it was gratifying to
have the first prize awarded to us.

During the past year you have carried on most
satisfactorily the work entrusted to you during the absence
abroad of Mr. Chase and myself, and during this fall when
Mr. Chase was absent three months during the trials of the
Elco MTB. The contract recently awarded to us by the Navy
calls for the greatest energy on your part in fulfilling the
same within the time limitation and seeing that the boats are
constructed and equipped in the very best possible manner.

In appreciation of the services that you have
rendered in the past I am enclosing herewith a check, and
take pleasure in further advising you, starting January 1st,
your salary will be at an increased amount, which we feel, due
to the responsibility which you will be called upon to carry,
is some reward for the services which you will be able to
render us.

In closing I wish to thank Mrs. Tremaine for the
attention and the service she has rendered us in the matter
of the interior decoration of the 57-footer. The color
scheme is most beautiful and the details of equipment will
certainly be admired by everyone.

Wishing you *and your family* a Very Merry Christmas and a Happy New
Year, I remain,

Yours very sincerely,

Henry R. Sutphen

Vice President

Figure 51. Original letter to Glenville S. Tremaine from Vice President
Henry R. Sutphen in 1939. The letter thanks Tremaine for a job well
done and mentions his added responsibilities while he and Irwin
Chase were abroad working on the MTBs. This was just before Elco
would purchase the Scott-Paine designed PT 9. (Frank J. Andruss Sr.
collection)

Editorial

Sponsored by
The Elco Works Employees'
War Service Fund Committee.

GREETINGS AND SALUTATIONS to each and every one of you from all of us here at Elco. At last we are able to comply with your many request letters for news from the home front. After a long detailed campaign to obtain your present addresses, beginning early in 1944, we have finally succeeded in completing our mailing files. You probably wondered how we, at home, managed to get your far-flung battle front addresses. For this we have to thank your mothers and fathers, brothers and sisters, wives and relatives for their cooperation in replying to more than 1000 postcards and letters, which we sent to them.

It is our hope that through the medium of this story and pictorial magazine we shall be able to bring to you interesting "Elco" home front news: something about management, production, sports, various events, how things are with us, in fact.

The entire center fold has been reserved exclusively for and dedicated to the Honor Roll with the latest addresses of all former Elco Workers in the Services. We believe this will enable many of you to get in touch with your Elco war buddies, and be helpful to those back home so they may be able to correspond with you.

On other pages you will find that we pay tribute to the men and women of the office, and those in the shop, who are contributing by their daily tasks the firm determination which inspires all with the same hope, the quick end of the war.

Then we have a resume of the highlights of events at Elco since December 7th, 1941— which takes in news of the plant; who's who in sports; descriptive progress of our Elco PT boats, and all the other things that might be of interest to you.

Dear Friends, we pray that you are in good health and spirits. We want you to know that we hold you constantly in our hearts, in our minds, and in our prayers. We know that you think of us, because your letters—and we have received more than 700 of them—testify to that fact. We want to thank all of you for these earnest and informative communications, which expressed deep appreciation of, and admiration for the Christmas packages we enjoyed sending. Each letter reflects the desire and expectation that we carry on with ever greater effort in producing the famed PT boats, and in doing everything within our power to hasten the end of the war, so that your task at the war front might end sooner and bring you home to us quicker.

In your honor, the Elco management has dedicated an Honor Roll tablet erected within the Naval Gate, displaying 1004 names. There is also a plaque upon which are the names of 27 of our former co-workers, in eternal remembrance of those who have paid the Supreme Sac-

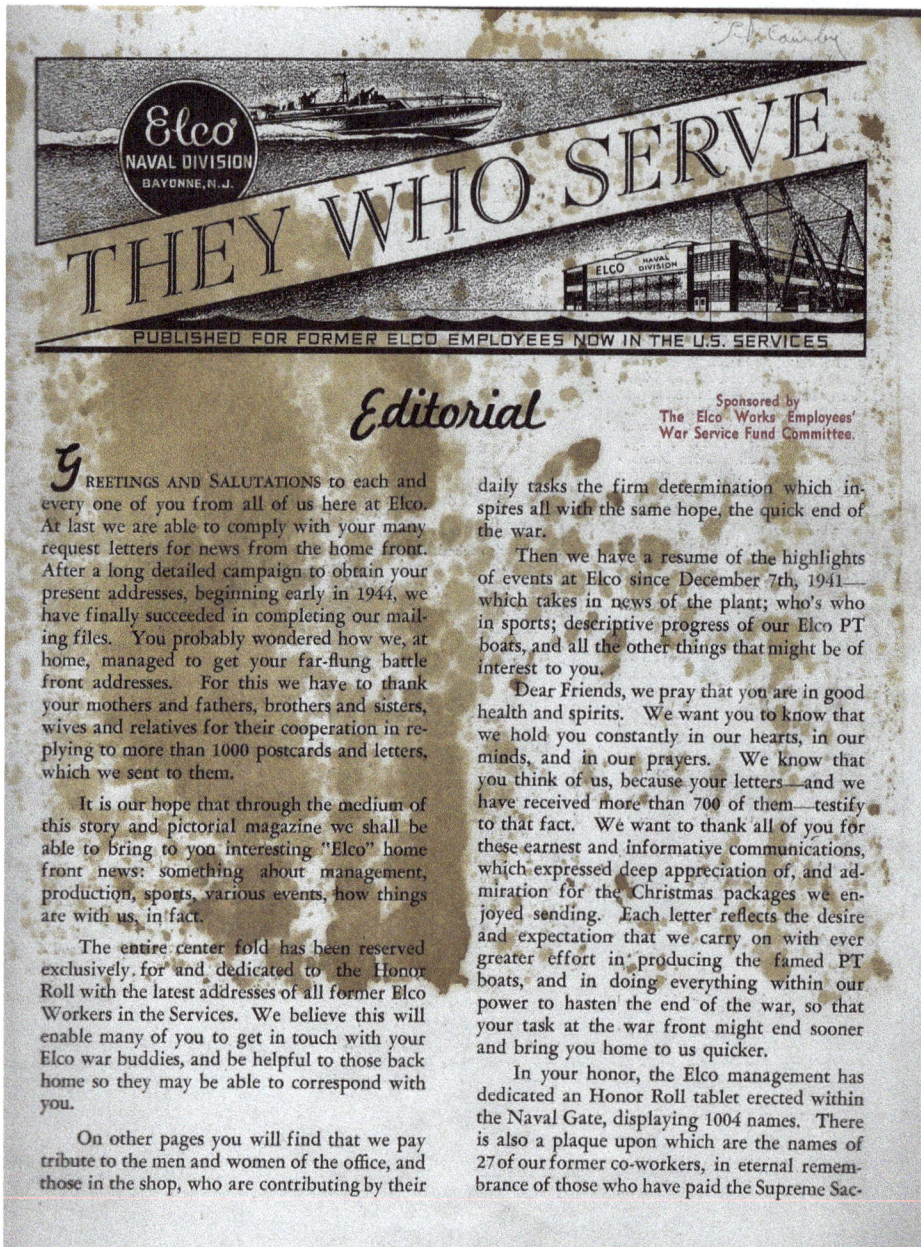

Figure 52. Late-war Elco publication of "They Who Serve", which highlighted those workers who started employment with Elco, then headed into different branches of the service. This one came out in 1945 close to the end of the war. (Frank J. Andruss Sr. collection)

Figure 53. The Elco Naval Division kept many of the squadron emblems at their factory, handing them out to officers and enlisted men that came to the plant to see how the boats were being made. Just about all of the operating squadrons had their own design although the early squadrons used the same design. These wonderful emblems were in fact decals that found their way on everything from tool boxes to the inside of the cabin areas of the boats. Here are two wonderful examples showing the mobile field unit and RON 25. (Frank J. Andruss Sr. collection)

Figure 54. Two more wonderful examples of Squadron emblems are these for RON 40 and RON 4. The RON 4 emblem was designed by a man named Peter Intrieri who was at the Motor Torpedo Boat Squadrons Training Center in 1943. The RON 4 Squadron, although designated for training, also maintained operational patrols. (Frank J. Andruss Sr. collection)

ELECTRIC BOAT COMPANY

445 PARK AVENUE
NEW YORK 22, N.Y.
ELdorado 5-3900

FOREWORD

It is with reluctance that we have concluded to dispose of the real estate of our Elco Yacht Division located in Bayonne, New Jersey, due to our discontinuing the manufacture of the Elco line of pleasure craft.

Since 1900, when we started operations in Bayonne, we have been well satisfied with the high quality of workers in all classifications whom we were able to recruit from this area, and likewise we fully appreciate the attitude of the City Authorities towards us and the cooperation they have given us.

The property is conveniently located on tidewater, served by rail and water, adjacent to an arm of New York Harbor and is close to main trucking arteries with easy access to tunnels and bridges.

We highly recommend this location to prospective purchasers and will be of all possible aid and assistance to them.

Yours very truly,

ELECTRIC BOAT COMPANY

(President)

Buildings No. 20 and No. 21

Figure 55. The sad end of the Elco Naval Division in Bayonne New Jersey came when the parent company, led by President of Electric Boat John J. Hopkins, made the decision to close the doors in 1949. This booklet pretty much tells the story by advertising the sale of the Bayonne plant. Hundreds of boats were turned out in Bayonne over the years and Elco produced some of the finest wooden boats of its time. (Frank J. Andruss Sr. collection)

Figure 56. Photo of Andrew Jackson Higgins, founder of Higgins Industries located in New Orleans. Higgins made 199 Higgins PT boats during World War Two. The company started out as a small boat-manufacturing business, and became one of the biggest companies in the world with upwards of eighty thousand workers and government contracts worth nearly three hundred fifty million dollars.

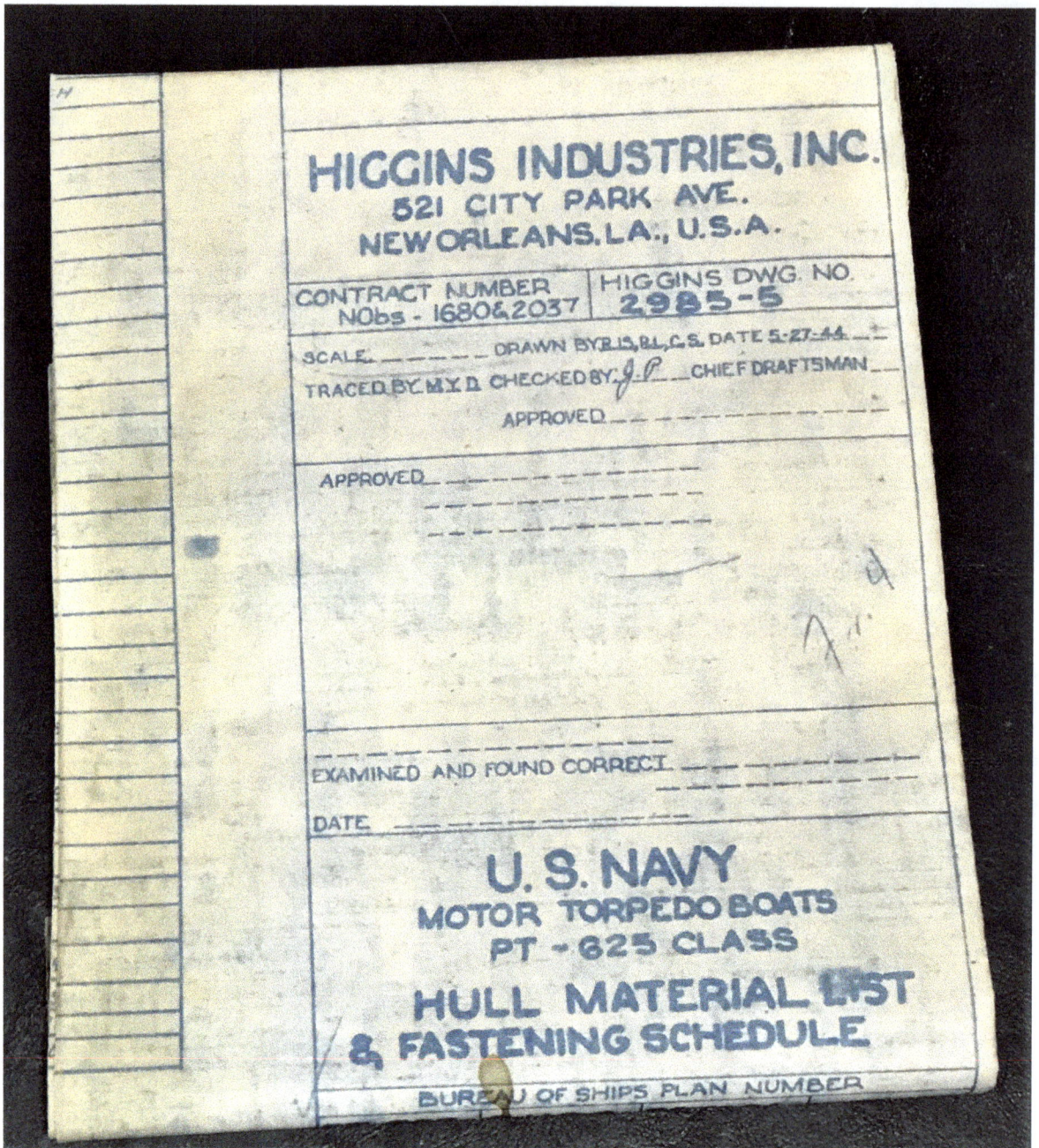

Figure 57. A Higgins Industries blueprint for the 625 series PT boat. This blueprint is showing the hull materials list and fastenings. (Save the PT Boat, Inc. collection)

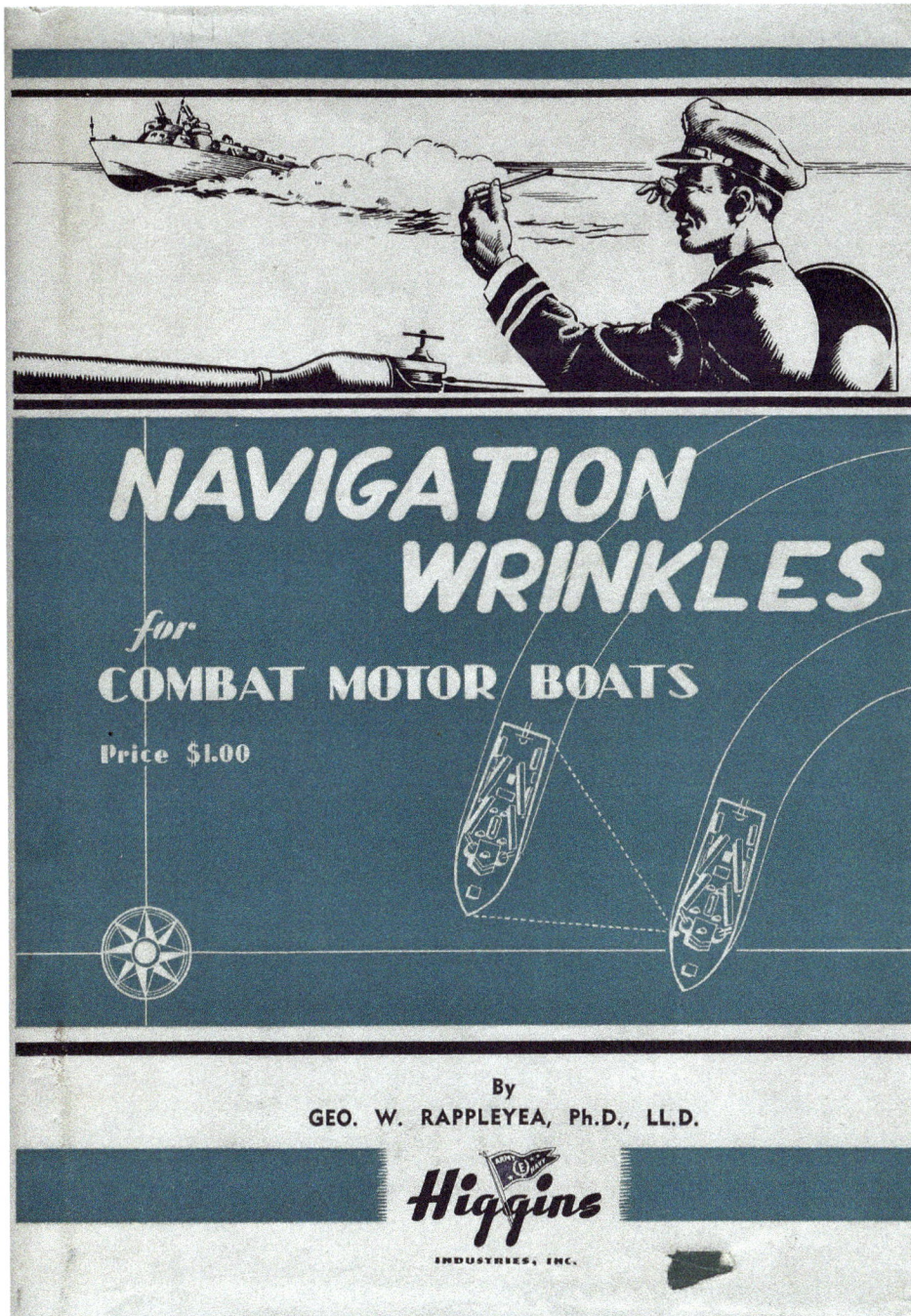

Figure 58. Higgins publication called "Navigation Wrinkles for Combat Motor Boats." Based upon lectures to students in previous classes of the Higgins boat operators and marine engine maintenance school. Published in 1944. (Frank J. Andruss Sr. collection)

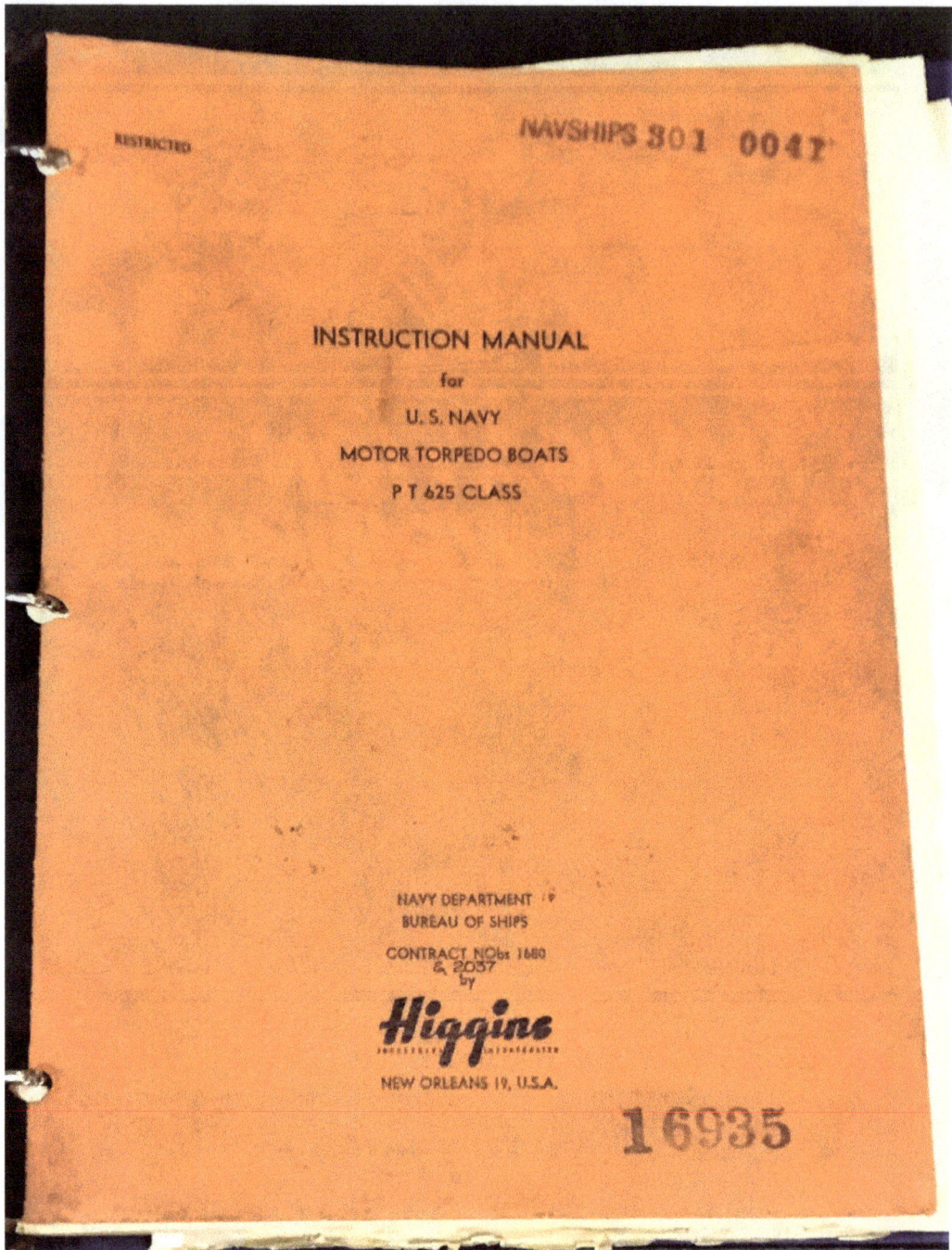

Figure 59. Instruction manual for the Higgins 625-class PT boat. Navy Department and the Bureau of Ships. (Save the PT Boat, Inc. collection)

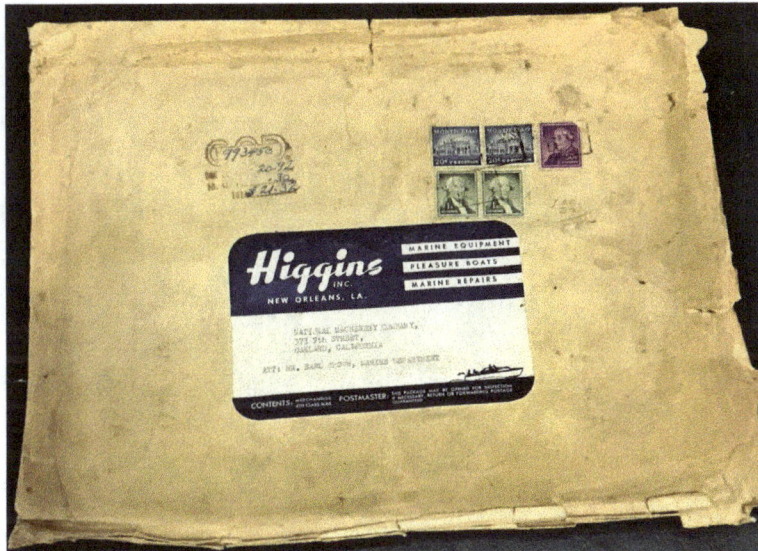

Figure 60. Rare example of an envelope that was sent from Higgins Industries to the National Machinery Company. (Save the PT Boat, Inc. collection)

Figure 61. Very rare example of a Higgins builder's plaque. This is from PT 93 which was scheduled to be shipped to the Soviet Union, but instead was shipped to the British where it was reclassified MTB 423. The boat operated in Italy with the British forces. (PT Boats Inc. collection)

Figure 62. Two Higgins builder's plates. The top one is very rare because it is from the Higgins Hellcat, which was PT 564, an experimental boat not selected for production. Bottom builder's plate is for PT-313 serving with RON 22. (PT Boats Inc. collection)

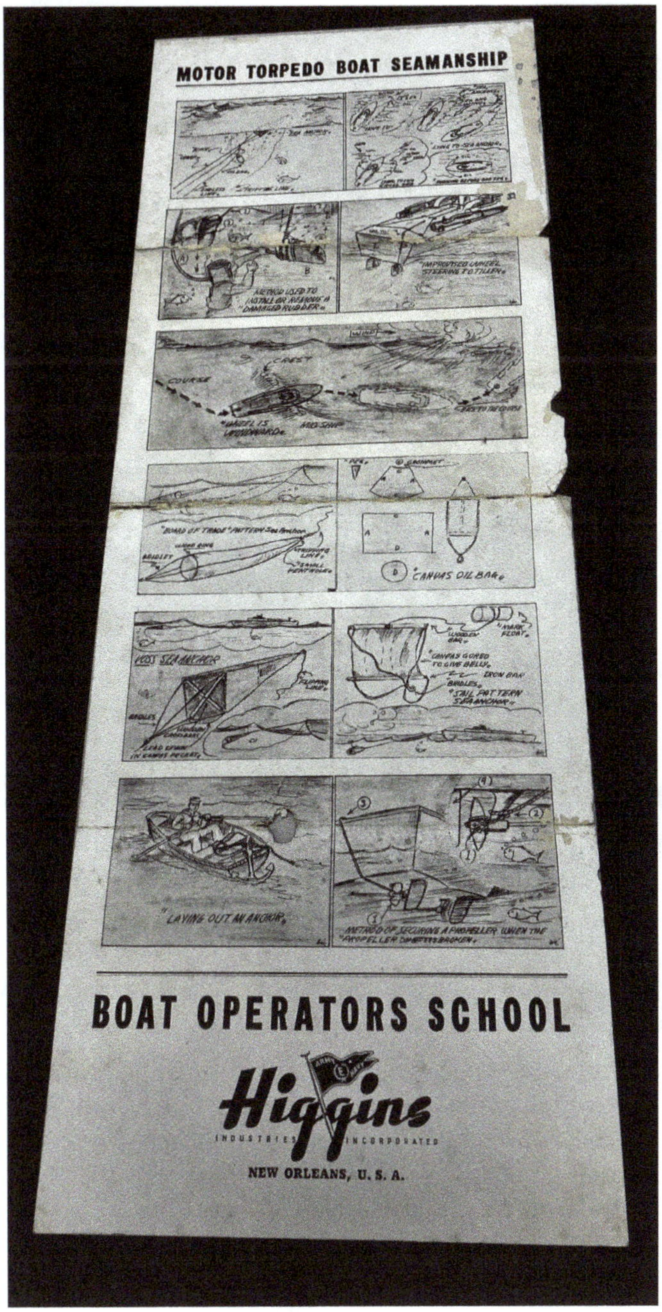

Figure 63. From the Higgins boat operator school is this cardboard poster for students. This one shows how to remove a damaged rudder, lay out the anchor, and secure a propeller when the prop shaft is broken. (Frank J. Andruss Sr. collection)

Figure 64. Frank P. Huckins was the founder of Huckins Yacht Corporation in Jacksonville Florida. The US Navy commissioned Huckins Yacht Corporation to build two squadrons of PT boats—a total of 18 boats—for service during World War II. The boats although not as popular as the Elco and the Higgins craft certainly had some wonderful qualities. They had a relatively high freeboard, with good headroom below the decks. A man could stand in the engine room, so engineers had plenty of space to work. Sleeping quarters on the Huckins PT vessels were considered to be comfortable by their captains and crews. They actually were a much better riding boat than the Elco and Higgins as they used a Quadraconic hull, a Huckins design in their construction. None of the Huckins boats saw combat during the war.

Figure 65. A wonderful Huckins factory model built by chief designer C. Raymond Teller. This model shows PT 95, a 78-footer that was completed in 1942. She carried two 21-inch torpedoes, eight depth charges, a stern mounted 20-mm gun and two.50-caliber gun tubs for twin machine guns. (Mystic Seaport collection)

Figure 66. A starboard look at the PT 95 factory model showing the unique design that set her apart from other PT boats.(Mystic Seaport collection)

Figure 67. Photo from the Huckins baseball team in 1944. The man in the front row and to the far right is William "Billy" Breedlove who worked as a carpenter with Huckins.

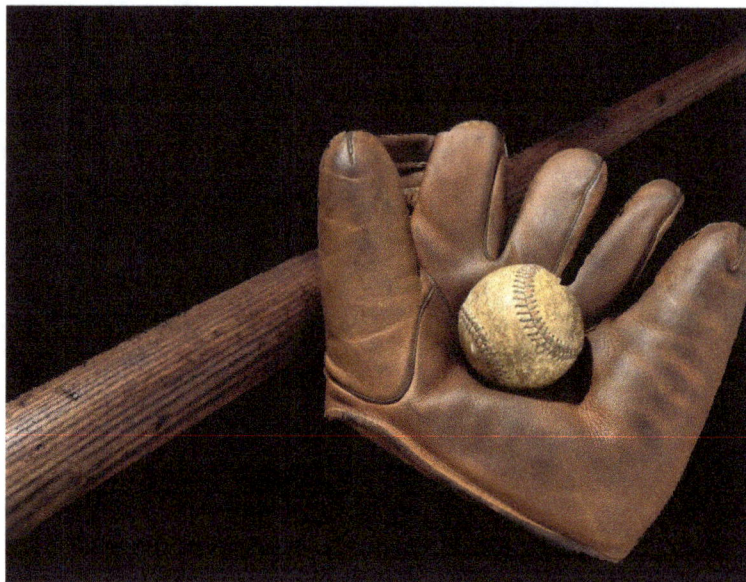

Figure 68. Baseball glove and bat that belonged to William Breedlove in the above photograph while playing on the Huckins baseball team. (Frank J. Andruss Sr. collection)

The Motor Torpedo Boat Squadrons Training Center (MTBSTC)

This base, located in Melville, Rhode Island, was the training base for those students who had originally joined up or were chosen for PT boat duty. The purpose of this base was to train personnel in the proper operation of the MTBs, and to prepare officers and enlisted men for duty in those boats. They would train them in operations, tactics, doctrine, and procedures. The base also offered much more, including a ship's store; a library; and officers' and enlisted men's clubs where they could relax without going into town. Dances and parties were available with the music mostly provided by a band made up of students. Sports were important to the life of the base and football, basketball, baseball, softball, boxing, swimming, and even bowling could be enjoyed. So much has been written about this base[1], but for our purposes we will be focusing on artifacts that made their way home as a reminder to those that were trained here during World War II.

---

[1] See, for example, *MTBSTC: Motor Torpedo Boat Squadrons Training Center* by Charles B. Jones (Nimble Books, 2011). ISBN: 978-1608880997.

Figure 69. Here is a photo of a painting that hung at the MTBSTC. It shows underway training on the boats while in formation, somewhere off Rhode Island. It offers a small look into what awaits both officer and enlisted men here at the base. They will learn communications, gunnery, seamanship, navigation, and engineering. Physical training will be tough but in the end they will be ready, and the knowledge gained here ever-lasting. Although New England winters were unforgiving and the ocean could be fierce at times, each student that trained here has a story to tell and remembers this base fondly.

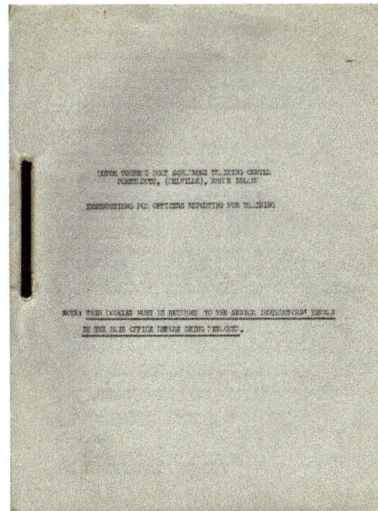

Figure 70. Original 1943 instructions for those student officers reporting for duty. This handbook contained information about the base and the training course. (Frank J. Andruss Sr. collection)

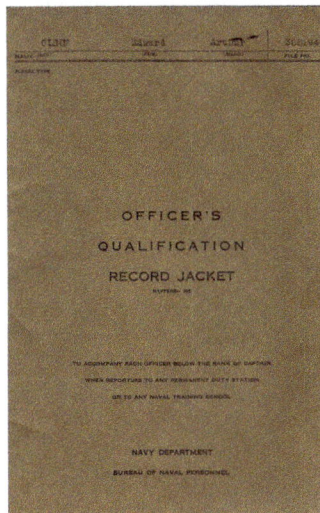

Figure 71. Original officers qualification report booklet that belonged to Lt. (j.g.) Edward A. Olson. He would complete his training here on May 16, 1942. In that same month he would report to RON 3 doing boat repair and riding some of the boats as a gunner. He returned to the MTBSTC in December of 1943 as an instructor. In March of 1944 he would again return to the Pacific as the hull officer on Base 35. He would once again make his way to the MTBSTC in June 1945 to become hull officer. (Frank J. Andruss Sr. collection)

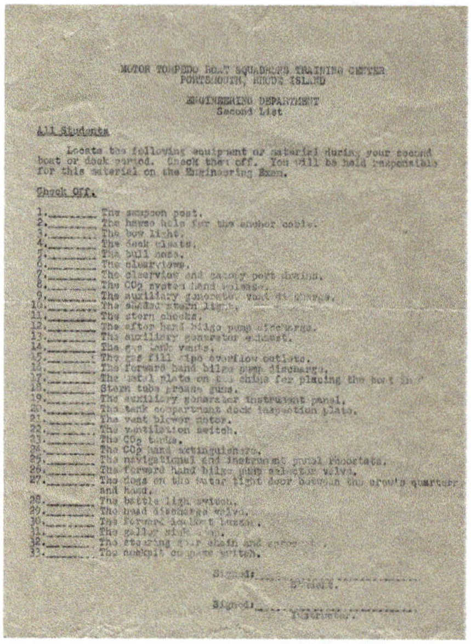

MOTOR TORPEDO BOAT SQUADRONS TRAINING CENTER
PORTSMOUTH, RHODE ISLAND

ENGINEERING DEPARTMENT
Second List

All Students

Locate the following equipment or material during your second boat or dock period. Check them off. You will be held responsible for this material on the Engineering Exam.

Check Off.

1.______ The sampson post.
2.______ The hawse hole for the anchor cable.
3.______ The bow light.
4.______ The deck cleats.
5.______ The bull nose.
6.______ The clearviews.
7.______ The clearview and canopy port drains.
8.______ The CO_2 system hand release.
9.______ The auxiliary generator vent [illegible].
10.______ The [illegible] stern light.
11.______ The stern chocks.
12.______ The after hand bilge pump discharge.
13.______ The auxiliary generator exhaust.
14.______ The gas tank vents.
15.______ The gas fill pipe overflow outlets.
16.______ The forward hand bilge pump discharge.
17.______ The metal plate on the chine for placing the boat in [illegible]
18.______ Stern tube grease guns.
19.______ The auxiliary generator instrument panel.
20.______ The tank compartment deck inspection plate.
21.______ The vent blower motor.
22.______ The ventilation switch.
23.______ The CO_2 tanks.
24.______ The CO_2 hand extinguishers.
25.______ The navigational and instrument panel rheostats.
26.______ The forward hand bilge pump selector valve.
27.______ The dogs on the water tight door between the crew's quarters and head.
28.______ The battle light switch.
29.______ The head discharge valve.
30.______ The forward [illegible] buzzer.
31.______ The galley [illegible].
32.______ The steering gear chain and [illegible].
33.______ The cockpit compass switch.

Signed:______________________
Student.

Signed:______________________
Instructor.

Figure 72. Engineering student check list. Students were responsible for checking off the enclosed items when on the PT boats. Later an exam would be given on this material. (Frank J. Andruss Sr. collection)

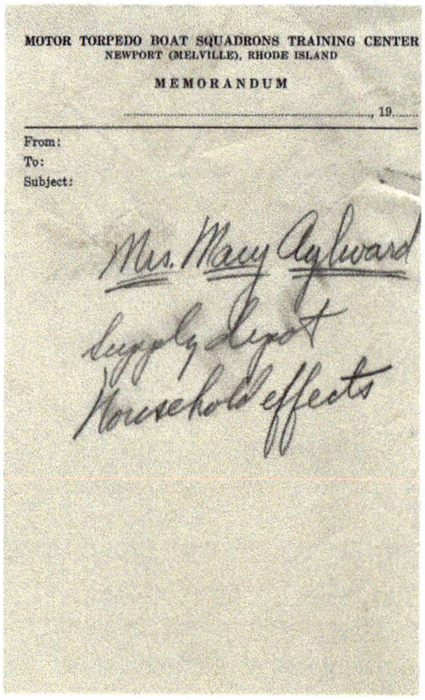

MOTOR TORPEDO BOAT SQUADRONS TRAINING CENTER
NEWPORT (MELVILLE), RHODE ISLAND

MEMORANDUM

________________, 19____

From:
To:
Subject:

Mrs. Mary Aylward
Supply Depot
Household effects

Figure 73. Memorandum pad from hull officer Lt. (j.g.) Edward A. Olson. He has penciled in some reminders. (Frank J. Andruss Sr. collection)

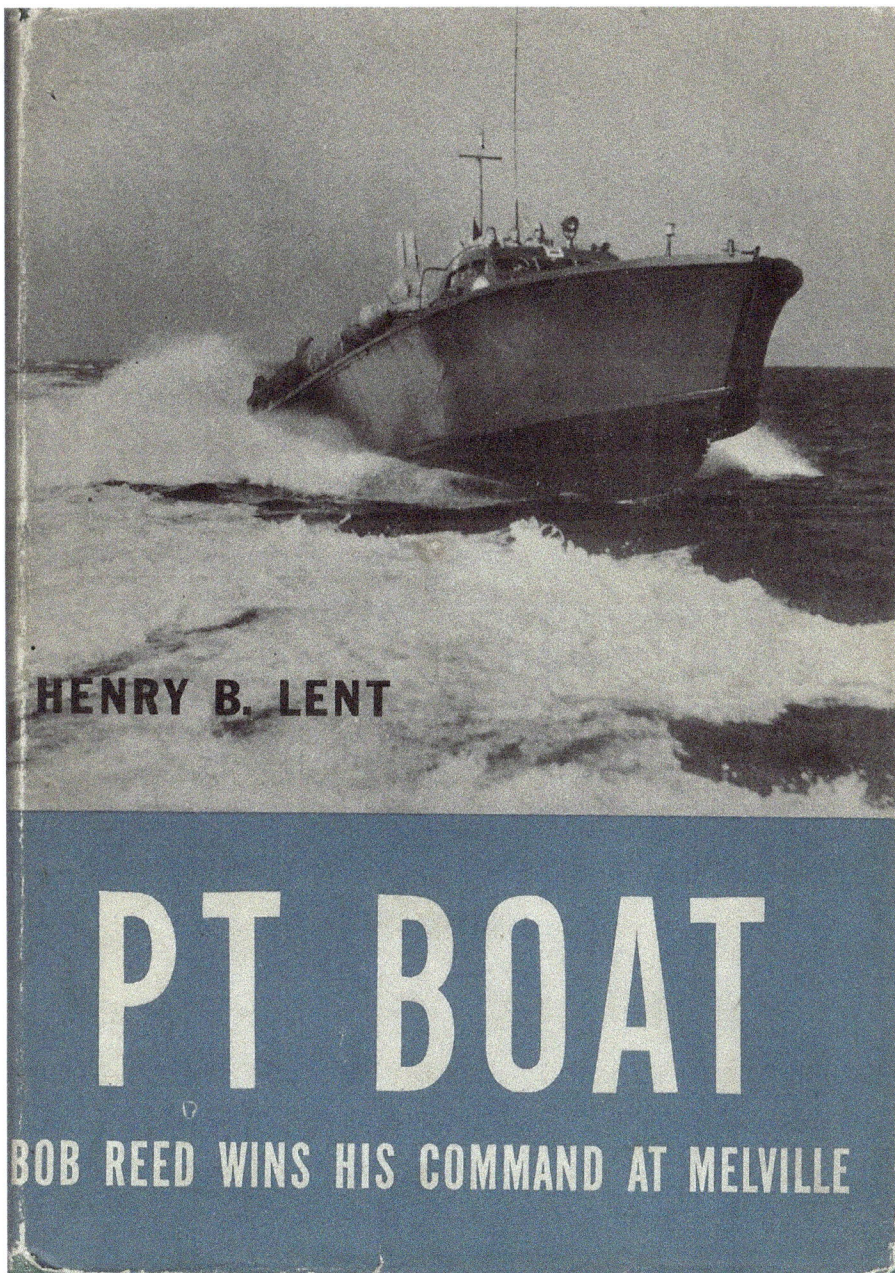

HENRY B. LENT

PT BOAT

BOB REED WINS HIS COMMAND AT MELVILLE

Figure 74. *PT Boat: Bob Reed wins his Command at Melville* (New York: MacMillan, 1943) was written by Henry B. Lent. It was the only book that featured the base as a major part of the story. The book follows Ensign Reed through his training until he gets his orders to report to an operating PT Boat Squadron. Back in 1943 this book sold for $2.00. (Frank J. Andruss Sr. collection)

Figure 75. Another publication called *The Annapolis of The Mosquito Fleet: Motor Torpedo Boat Squadron Training Center* was pretty much a war-time souvenir picture book. It was about the base and was generally carried in the ship's store. It was usually sent home to the family so they could see the activities going on at the base. This was published in mid-1944. (Frank J. Andruss Sr. collection)

Figure 76. Here is a photo showing just how harsh the winter months could be while attending the MTBSTC. Going from class to class in these conditions was pretty tough, not to mention any underway training on the boats. Special gear for the winter was given to all student officers and enlisted men, including foul weather gear. (Frank J. Andruss Sr. collection)

Figure 77. A wonderful example of a foul weather jacket that was used at the base during the harsh winter months. Going from class to class at the base in the winter could be extremely cold, not to mention the brutal cold while conducting underway training on the boats. This jacket belonged to GM1/c Wallace McNeish who was a student at Melville in 1942. (Frank J. Andruss Sr. collection)

Figure 78. Underway training about to begin on PT 545 with RON 4, showing the wool face masks being worn to guard against the cold.

Figure 79. During cold weather months underway training on the boats could be brutal. Because of the winter months of New England many of these training exercises would be canceled. Patrols however continued and being warm was on everyone's mind. Here we see the Navy standard early winter face mask and helmet. The mask was made of wool and the helmet was made from a blue jungle cloth with a wool lining. This set was used at the Base and worn while on PT 100. (PT Boats Inc. collection)

Figure 80. From the ship's store, this is a rare example of Gobby the Goat, a wonderful stuffed toy reminiscent of the modern craze for Beanie Babies™. Made by the Intercollegiate Press Co. in Kansas City, these were purchased by those at the base as gifts for loved ones back home. These stuffed goats (the Navy's mascot) represented MTBSTC and the Fuel and Net Depot. (PT Boats Inc. collection)

Figure 81. Another look at Gobby the Goat. (PT Boats Inc. collection)

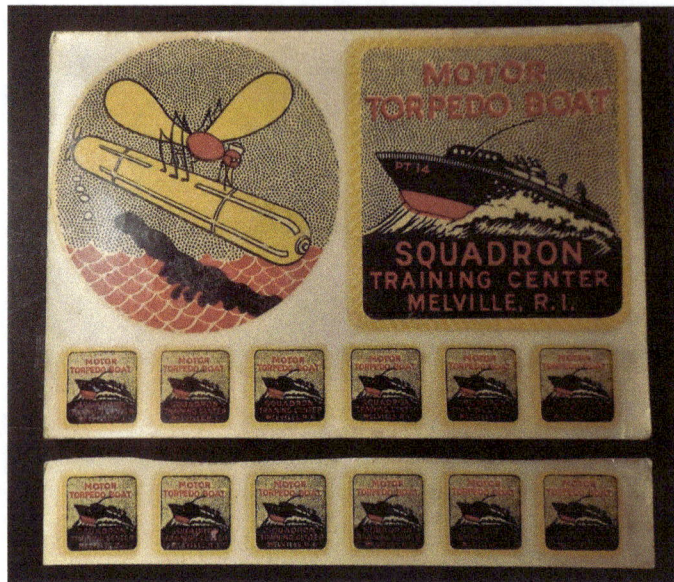

Figure 82. Another fun item that could be purchased at the ship's store was this MTBSTC decal set. In the set we see the Mosquito Fleet emblem and the MTBSTC decal with PT 14 riding a huge wave. (Frank J. Andruss Sr. collection)

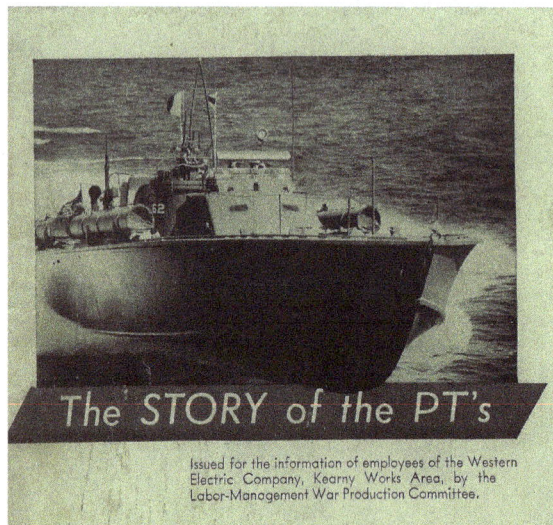

Figure 83. Although an Elco publication this little book, "The STORY of the PT's" was made available at the ship's store and featured an inside look at the building and story of the Elco PT boats. (Frank J. Andruss Sr. collection)

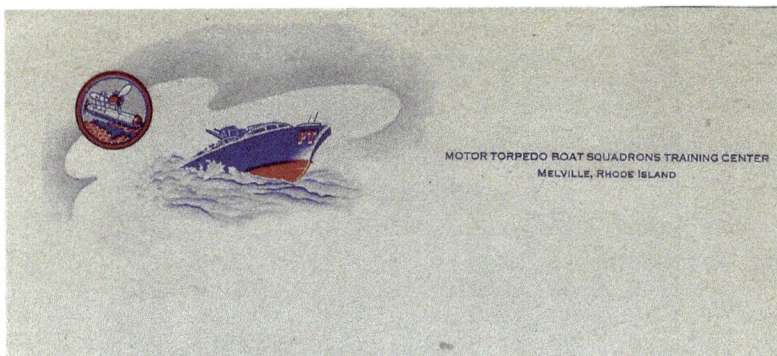

Figure 84. A pristine example of one style of MTBSTC letterhead used to write letters home to loved ones. This style has several vivid colors showing PT 14 crashing through the waves. (Frank J. Andruss Sr. collection)

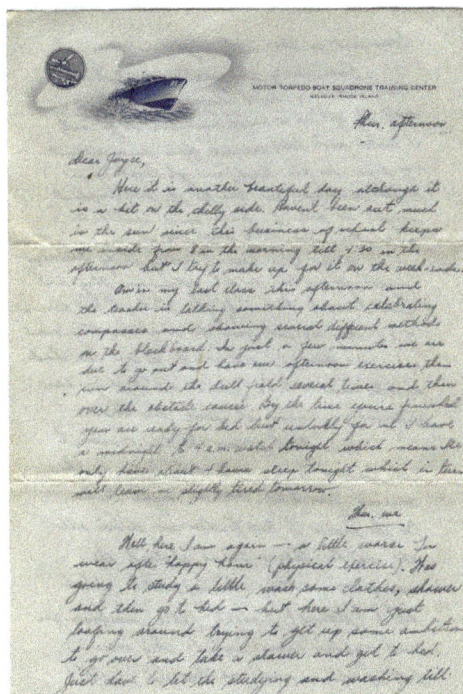

Figure 85. This is the second style letterhead from the MTBSTC and as you can see has been written on. This Navy blue color style, although not as colorful as the first, served the purpose. (Frank J. Andruss Sr. collection)

Figure 86. The MTBSTC formed their own fire department, inviting volunteers from existing personnel to man the department. This photo shows Fire Chief Allan Lawrence Sr. USN posing by one of the departments pumper trucks. (Frank J. Andruss Sr. collection)

Figure 87. Original fire department helmet that was once worn by Allan Lawrence Sr. before he became Fire Chief at the base. Rare and hard to find. Note the white paint at the very top of the helmet signifies a certain fire department code. (Frank J. Andruss Sr. collection)

Figure 88. A look at the original MTBSTC fire department first aid box marked "M.T.B." and "Medical" on the box. It is painted Fire Department Red. (Allan Lawrence Jr. collection)

Figure 89. A look into the medical first aid box showing that the contents are still intact after 75 years. Inside we see battle dressing, several compresses, tourniquets and other medical items that could be used for emergencies at the base. (Allan Lawrence Jr. collection)

Figure 90. A look at a very rare MTBSTC Fire Department No. 2 early badge. This badge would be worn by those that worked on the Fire Department while on duty. (Frank J. Andruss Sr. collection)

Figure 91. Example of an extremely rare MTBSTC police badge, likely from the Master at Arms force at the base. (Frank J. Andruss Sr. collection)

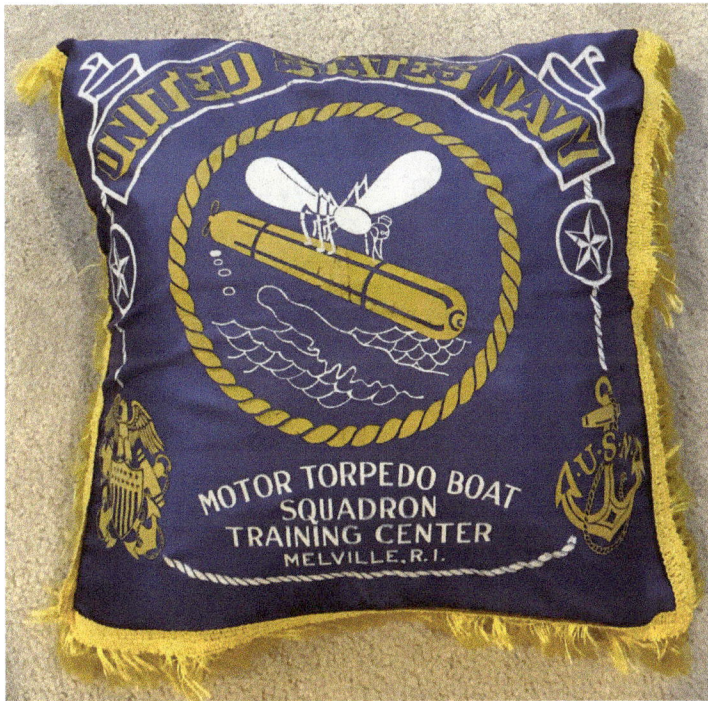

Figure 92. A wonderful example of what would be known as the "sweetheart pillow." These pillows were available in the ship's store. Made from a silk material they had the Mosquito Fleet emblem on the cover and the name of the base. Just the cover was sold but many would insert a pillow inside where it could be used anywhere in the home. (Frank J. Andruss Sr. collection)

Figure 93. A very nice example of a women's handkerchief that was available in the ship's store. (Frank J. Andruss Sr. collection)

Figure 94. Sports were a large part of the MTBSTC. Many who played sports before on high school or college teams continued playing while at the base. This photo shows members of the football team. Twenty-one players on the this team were returning combat vets. This team would play in the Harvard game on November 11, 1944. They would go on to defeat Harvard 13-0.

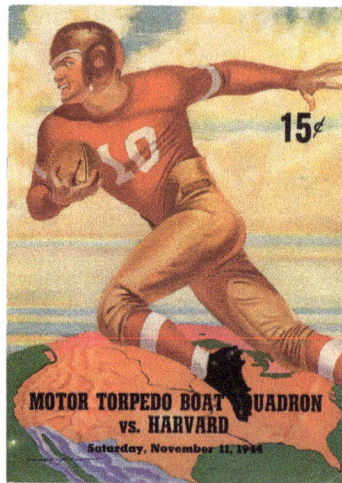

Figure 95. Harvard football program for a game billed as Motor Torpedo Boat Squadron vs. Harvard on November 11, 1944. (Frank J. Andruss Sr. collection)

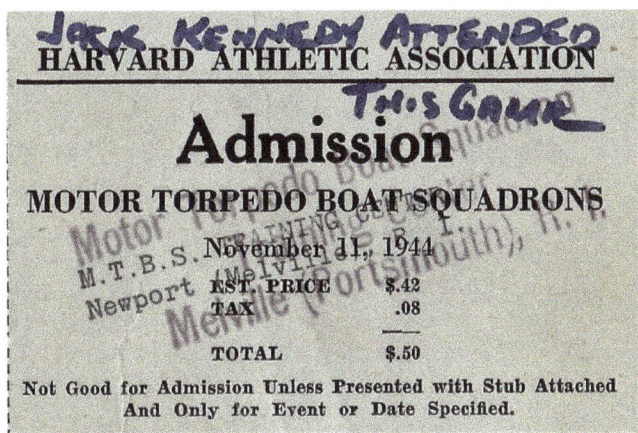

Figure 96. Original Harvard ticket for the November 11th game from the Harvard Athletic Association. MTBSTC football team member Lt. (j.g.) Stan Smith wrote on the ticket that John F. Kennedy attended this game. (Frank J. Andruss Sr. collection)

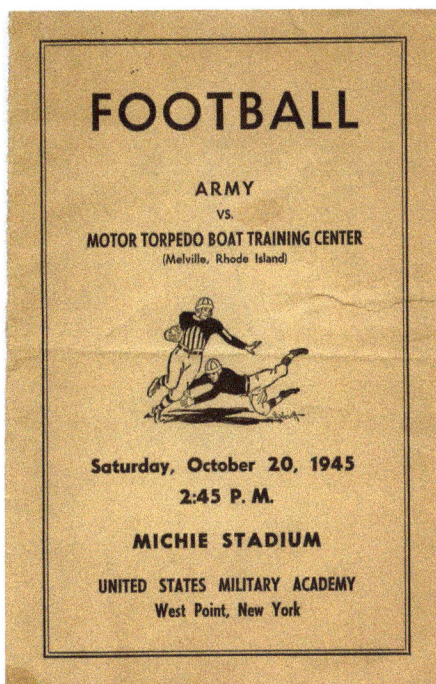

Figure 97. Football program for Army vs. Motor Torpedo Boat Training Center. This game was played at Michie Stadium on October 20, 1945. The MTBSTC would lose this game 55- 13. (Alex Johnson collection)

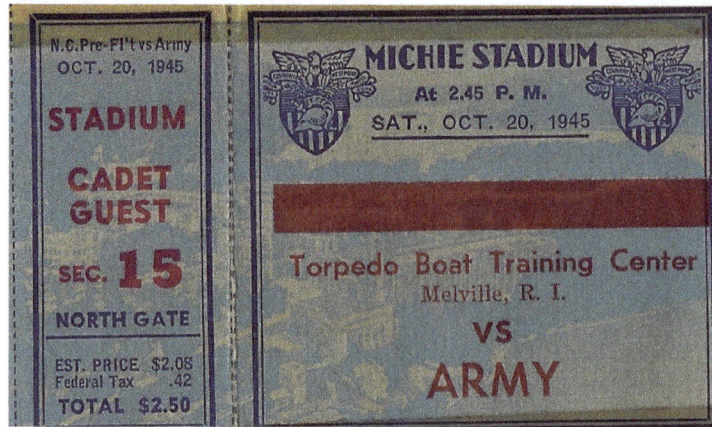

Figure 98. Unused football ticket to the Army vs. Motor Torpedo Boat Training Center. (Frank J. Andruss Sr. collection)

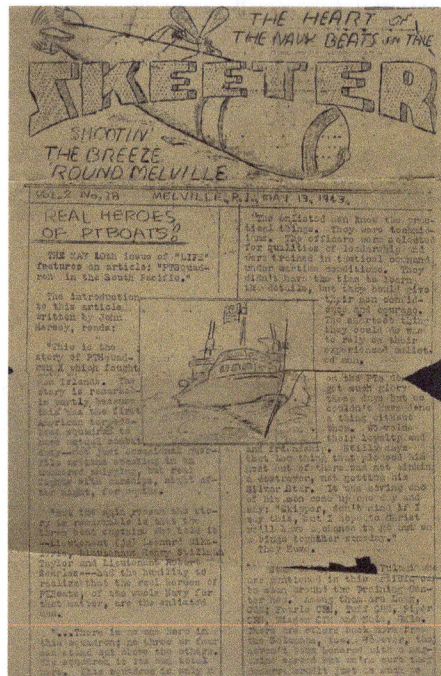

Figure 99. *The Skeeter* was the MTBSTC's weekly newsletter that was printed and distributed to the men's living quarters every Thursday. It usually consisted of 8 to 10 pages of insight on the base. It carried events that took place on the base, war news, sports scores, movie schedules, promotions and much more. This example came out on May 13, 1943. (Frank J. Andruss Sr. collection)

Figure 100. Another example of *The Skeeter,* which came out on March 16, 1944. This paper was not printed on cheaper mimeographed paper like others, but on higher quality paper and was printed at Camp Endicott at the Seabee base in Narragansett Bay. These better quality newspapers were usually done on the week of the anniversaries of the MTBSTC's commissioning and the start of the newsletter, March 16 and November 26. (Frank J. Andruss Sr. collection)

Figure 101. Dances and parties were usually held after each class completed its course, at the base or at local establishments. One favored venue was Carpenters Hall, located in Newport Rhode Island not far from the base. Wife's and girlfriends attended these parties.

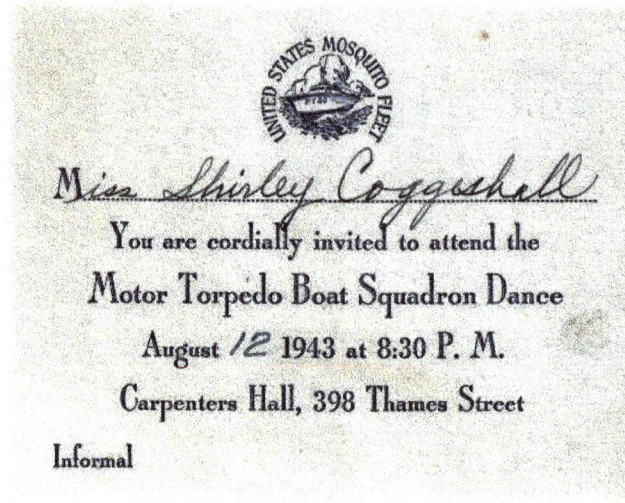

Figure 102. Invitation made out to Shirley Coggeshell to attend The Motor Torpedo Boat Squadron Dance on August 12, 1943. It was to be held at Carpenters Hall and it was informal. (Frank J. Andruss Sr. collection)

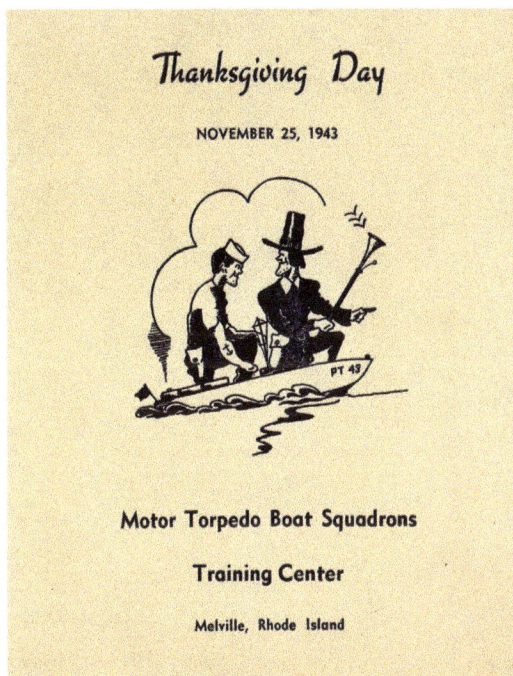

Figure 103. A very nice example of the MTBSTC Thanksgiving Day Menu for November 25, 1943. (Frank J. Andruss Sr. collection)

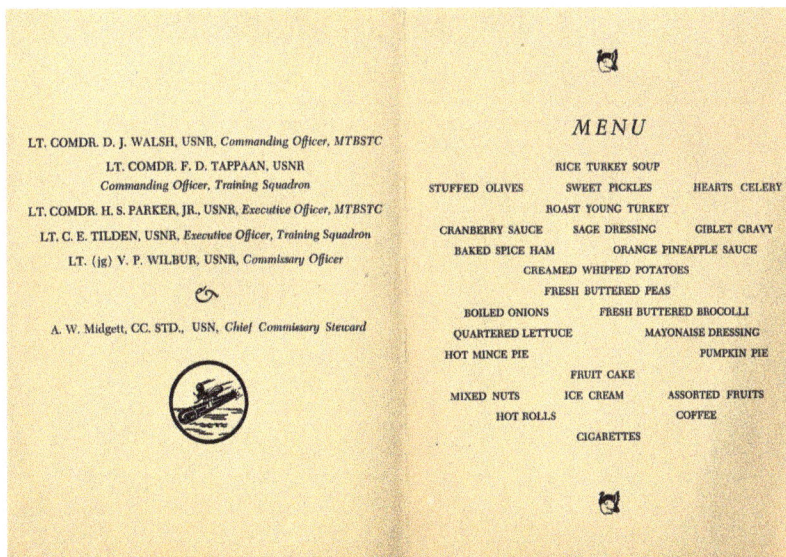

Figure 104. From the looks of the menu, the boys at the base had a fine Thanksgiving dinner with all of the fixings. (Frank J. Andruss Sr. collection)

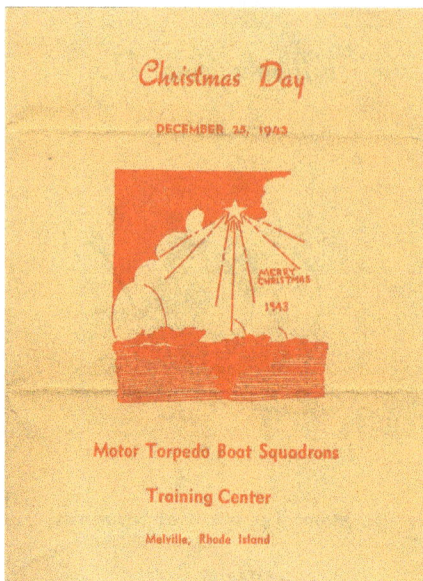

Figure 105. Christmas Dinner Menu at the MTBSTC base for December 25, 1943. A very nice color red showing PT boats under the star of Bethlehem. (Frank J. Andruss Sr. collection)

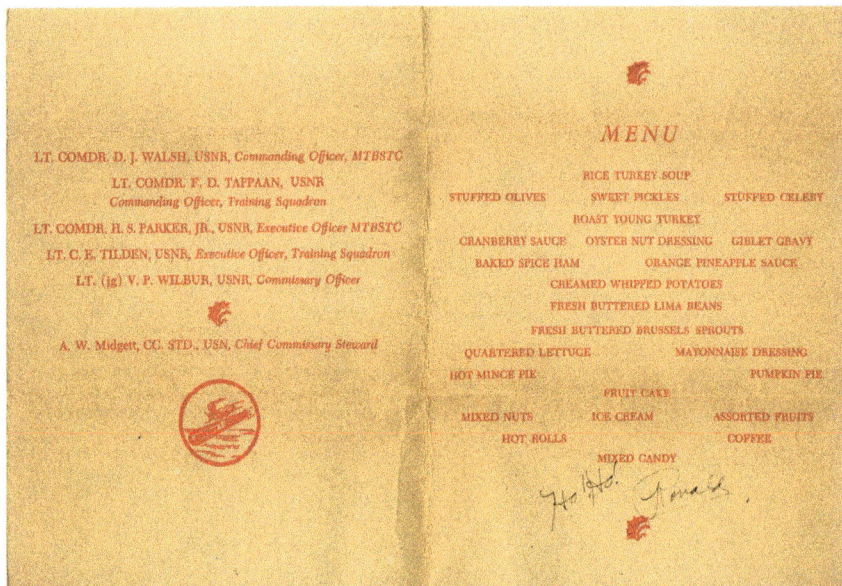

Figure 106. From the looks of the inside of the menu the food served this day was fit for a king. With roast young turkey, baked spice ham, and all the fixings, no one left the mess hall hungry. (Frank J. Andruss Sr. collection)

Figure 107. Joseph Alex Michaud had a long career in the Navy. Young Lt. Michaud was assigned to the dynamometer laboratories of Packard Motor Car Company, where he helped to raise the horsepower of the Packard engines from 900 to 1350, which was needed to propel the early Elco 70-footers. Shortly after, Lt. Michaud was transferred to the Motor Torpedo Boats Squadrons Training Center, becoming head of the engineering department. He went out on many of RON 4's patrols. Lt. Michuad became the technical adviser for the Bureau of Ships as it developed sound and slide motion pictures to train personnel in using the PT boat against the enemy. (Frank J. Andruss Sr. collection)

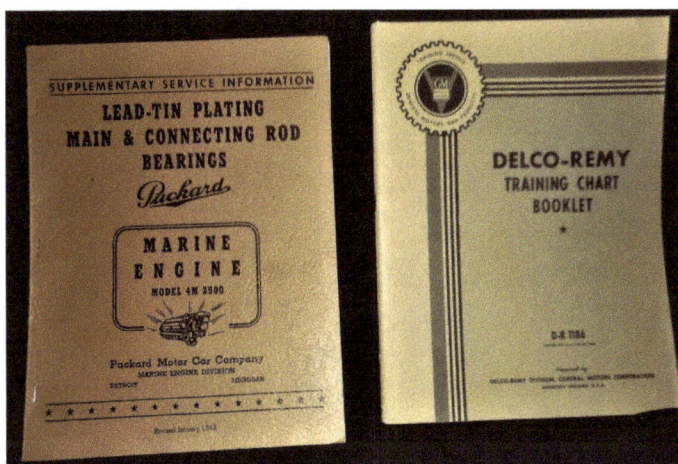

Figure 108. Two different manuals from the Michaud collection that were used while he was at MTBSTC. (Frank J. Andruss Sr. collection)

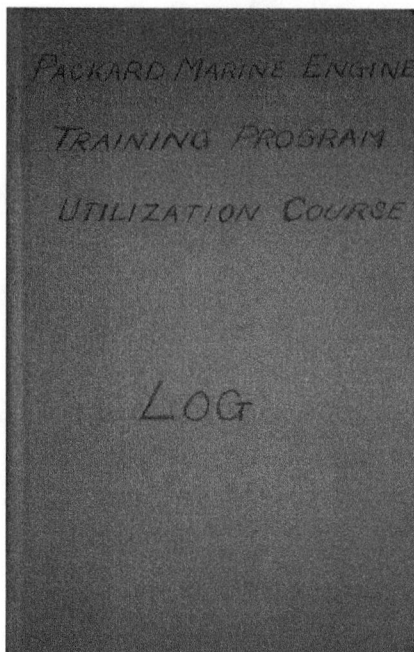

Figure 109. Log book from Michaud titled "Packard Marine Engine Training Program Utilization Course" (Frank J. Andruss Sr. collection)

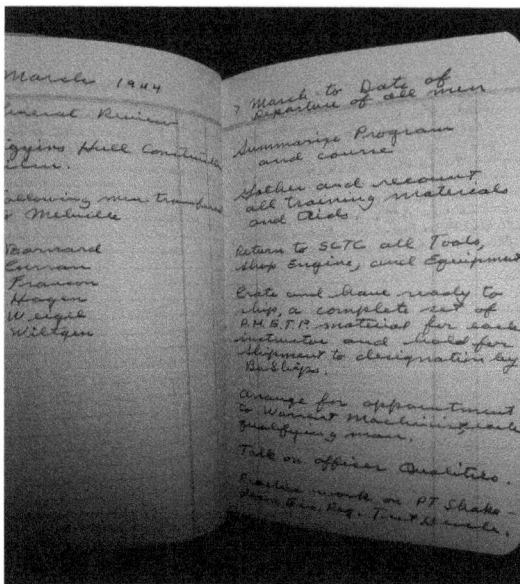

Figure 110. Inside look at Michaud's log book with entries from March of 1944. (Frank J. Andruss Sr. collection)

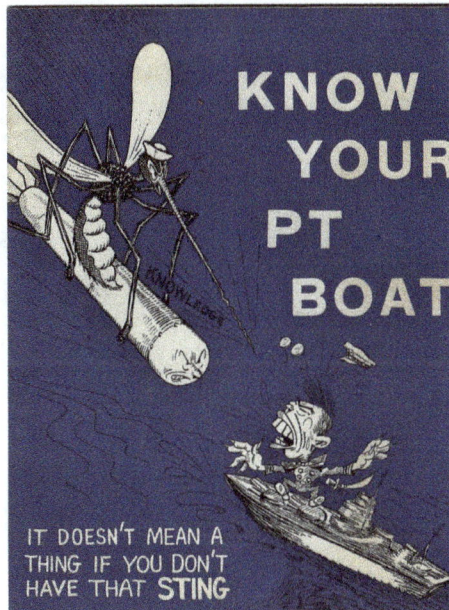

Figure 111. "Know Your PT Boat," July 1945, was created very near the end of World War II to use as an introduction to PT boats for crews in training. (Frank J. Andruss Sr. collection)

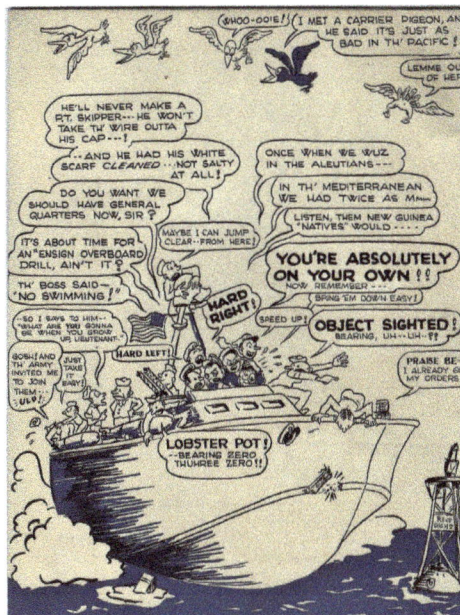

Figure 112. Back cover of the book showing a comical cartoon with many sayings. (Frank J. Andruss Sr. collection)

Figure 113. The day that all officers and enlisted men at the base looked forward to: graduation, where all the hard work and instruction pays off. In this photo taken at the PT Boat Auditorium, it is crowded with enlisted sailors from one of the classes, as well as officers who are getting their certificates of graduation and occupy the front row of seats. Giving out the certificates is Lt. Cdr. Walsh, the Commanding Officer of the base.

Figure 114. This is one of the MTBSTC graduation certificates for William C. Moen, Motor Machinist Mate second class. (Frank J. Andruss Sr. collection)

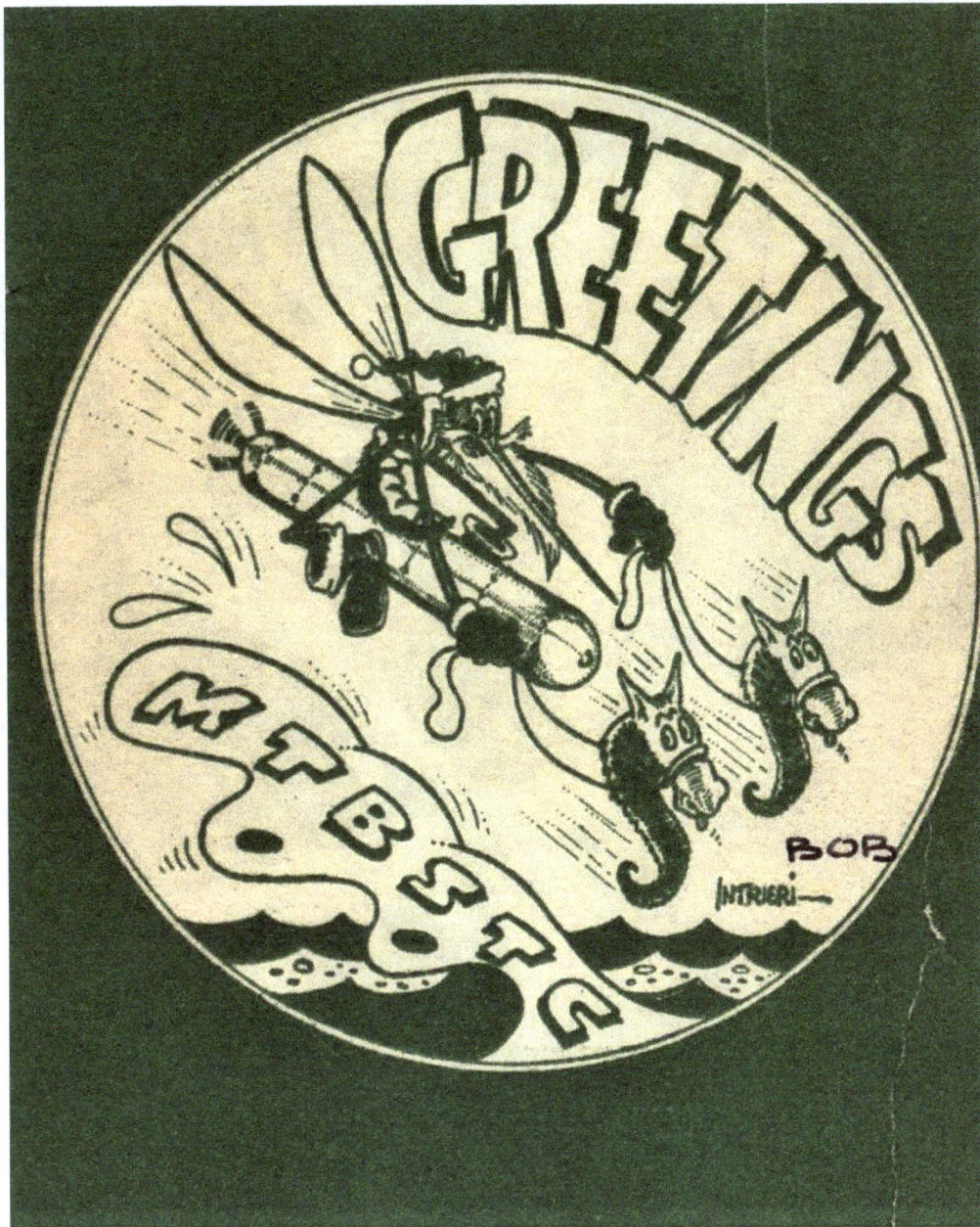

Figure 115. A rare Christmas greeting card from the base. The graphics for this card was done by storekeeper Peter Intrieri who was stationed at the base in late 1943 after being assigned to RON2. His artistic talent was recognized and he also did the art work for the RTU (Repair Training Unit) among other work. (Frank J. Andruss Sr. collection)

Figure 116. RON 4 dance booklet from 1945, one of several dances that was held on the base at the drill hall. The PT Swingsters, a dance band made up of those at the base provided the music. Meals were usually eaten at the mess hall before the dance. Brought home by RM1/c William E. Paul.

ARTIFACTS FROM THE FRONT

The PT boats of World War II operated from the Pacific Ocean to the Aleutians. Daily they would fight it out with enemy ships, planes, shore batteries, and barges. There is no doubt that the war affected the lives of every PT boater and the artifacts they collected can relate amazing and haunting stories. In the Pacific there was an efficient and beneficial barter system in place between the sailors and the locals. Items were traded for trinkets and even fresh bananas. Many of these trinkets made it home or were sent home to loved ones. It is easy to understand the love one can have for one's boat: after all these little PT boats were home to these young boys for several years. It was not uncommon to remove a flag or a builder's plate from the boat, as something to remind one of the time spent on her. In this section we will take a look at some of those items that came home from the front and meant so much to the crews.

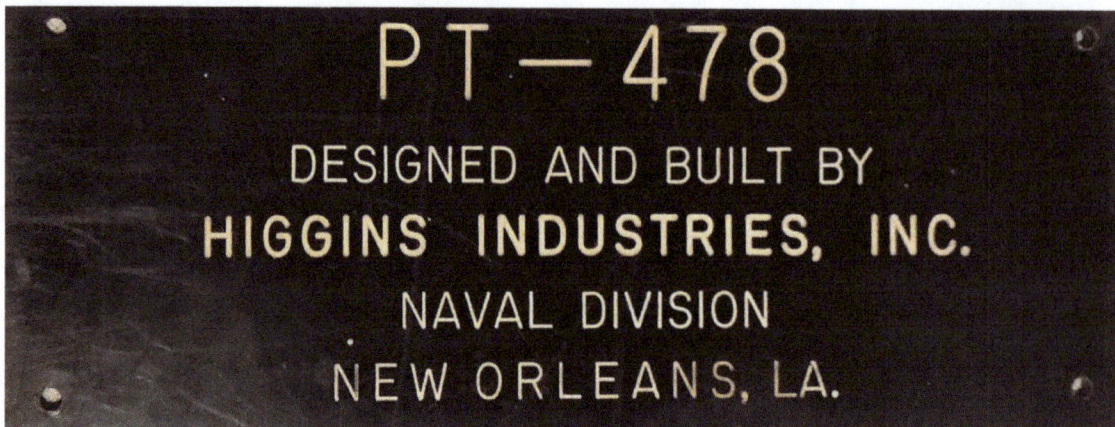

Figure 117. A wonderful example of a HIggins PT boat builder's plate. This one belonged to PT 478 which served with RON 32. These builder's plates would often find their way into a crew members sea bag as mementos. (Save the PT Boat, Inc. collection)

Figure 118. Another rare item sometimes taken home was the boat bell. This fine example was from Higgins PT 481 which served with RON 32. Her home is now on the bridge of restored Higgins PT 658 in Portland, Oregon. (Save the PT Boat, Inc. collection)

Figure 119. A nice example of the battle flag from PT 221, removed from the boat by Ens. William T. Robinson. Notice the ends of the flag have been tattered by the wind whipping through it. (Frank J. Andruss Sr. collection)

Figure 120. This example shows the battle flag and commissioning pennant from PT 216. This was brought home by crewman William C. Moen Momm1/c. (Frank J. Andruss Sr. collection)

Figure 121. Francis J. Napolillo, ship's cook, served in the early days of World War Two with Motor Torpedo Boat Squadron 3 under the command of Lt. John D. Bulkeley in the Philippines. They were credited with the rescue of General Douglas MacArthur who was whisked away from Corregidor and the oncoming Japanese. These little PTs were the only Navy available at that time. Napolillo served on PT 35 until the boat was lost, and he headed for the hills. He fought under Wendell W. Fertig with the Philippine guerrillas and was later taken from the Philippines to Perth Hospital in Australia on the submarine USS *Bowfin*.

Figure 122. Items that belonged to Francis J. Napolillo while with RON 3 and the Philippine resistance. (Frank J. Andruss Sr. collection)

Figure 123. Knifes obtained by Francis J. Napolillo while in the Philippines. (Frank J. Andruss Sr. collection)

Figure 124. Original Silver Star and box presented to Francis J. Napolillo "for extraordinary heroism and distinguished service in the line of his profession while serving with Motor Torpedo Boat Squadron THREE (MTB-3), from 11 to 13 March 1942, in the Philippine Islands during a extraordinary action in a retrograde maneuver involving General Douglas MacArthur.." (Frank J. Andruss Sr. collection)

Figure 125. Reverse of the Silver Star presented to Francis J. Napolillo. This was actually an Army Silver Star that was presented by General Douglas MacArthur while Napolillo was in the Hospital. MacArthur's staff had it engraved before it was presented. (Frank J. Andruss Sr. collection)

Figure 126. A fine example of this RON 15 hand-painted plaque which was removed from PT 204. Brought home by crewmen David V. Prentice. (Save the PT Boat, Inc. collection)

Figure 127. Fine example of a 1911.45 pistol with Navy sheath and belt. The.45 was a prized side arm that was carried on all US Navy PT boats. (Wally Boerger collection)

Figure 128. A fine example of a 10-gauge flare gun with Holster and storage belt. This was taken home after the war by GM Frank Lesage who served on PT 205. (Save the PT Boat, Inc. collection)

Figure 129. Japanese sword that was brought back from the Philippines. These were always in top demand for PT crews to try and obtain. Brought home by QM John W. Hughes. (Frank J. Andruss Sr. collection)

Figure 130. Photo of Lt. Cmdr. Alan R. Montgomery. During the summer of 1942, he was placed in command of Motor Torpedo Boat Squadron 3. Their destination was the Solomon Islands, where they were the first PT boat squadron to take part in the fierce naval and air battle that raged on the islands and in the straits around Guadalcanal. For his service during World War II, Montgomery was awarded the Silver Star, Legion of Merit, a Gold Star in lieu of a second Legion of Merit; a Bronze Star, Combat Victory Medal, and a Philippine Liberation Medal with two Bronze Stars. (Frank J. Andruss Sr. collection)

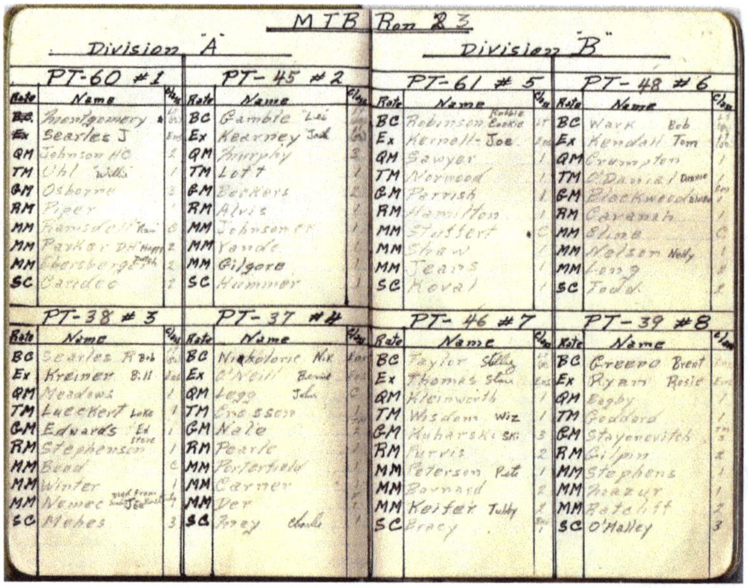

Figure 131. Original pocket notebook that Montgomery brought home showing the two PT divisions he was in charge of and a list of the boats and those onboard. (Frank J. Andruss Sr. collection)

Figure 132. Temporary citation signed by Admiral Halsey and presented to Lt. Cmdr. Alan R. Montgomery for his actions in the Solomons on October 13, 1942. In this case is his original Silver Star. (Frank J. Andruss Sr. collection)

Figure 133. Typical battle lantern that was used by the Navy and the PT boats. These would also find their way home on occasion. (Wally Boerger collection)

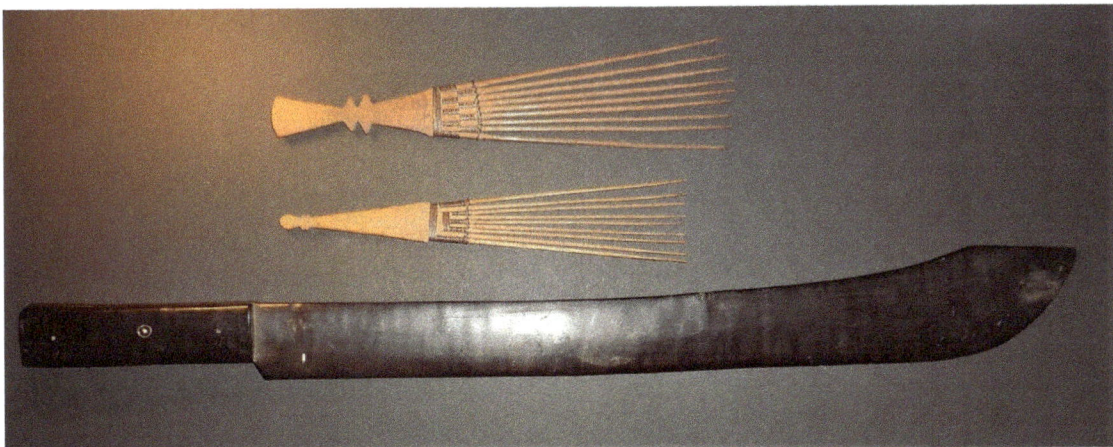

Figure 134. Items brought home by Don Macbeth who was stationed at Milne Bay, Papua New Guinea during World War II. Don worked doing overhaul on the 4M-2500 Packard marine engines. Here we see a hand-carved machete type made from a rare black wood and two Native combs. (Frank J. Andruss Sr. collection)

Figure 135. A fine example of a Japanese Nambu Type 14 pistol and holster. Taken home by ship's cook 1/c Eugene Samuel Mossberger who served with RON 24. (Save the PT Boat, Inc. collection)

Figure 136. A 37-mm flare gun taken home by Torpedoman Jack Duncan who served on PT 103. (Save the PT Boat, Inc. collection)

Figure 137. A wonderful example of an M-1 Carbine 30-caliber semi-automatic rifle complete with gun cover. Certainly a weapon that would be a part of the PT boat's armament. (Wally Boerger collection)

Figure 138. A nice example of the 1903 Springfield rifle that would find their way onto the PT boats. This was a five round magazine bolt action rifle. One might find this type of weapon used more with the early boats of the Philippine campaign, as it was replaced with the much faster firing eight round M-1 Garand rifle. (Save the PT Boat, Inc. collection)

Figure 139. A wonderful color photo of Andrew Jackson Kirksey Torpedoman 2/c. Kirksey would serve with RON 2 onboard PT 109 under command of Lt. (j.g.) John F. Kennedy. This photo was taken near his boot camp training station in Norfolk, Virginia. Kirksey, along with shipmate Harold W. Marney, was lost when their PT boat was rammed by the Japanese destroyer *Amagiri* on August 2, 1943.

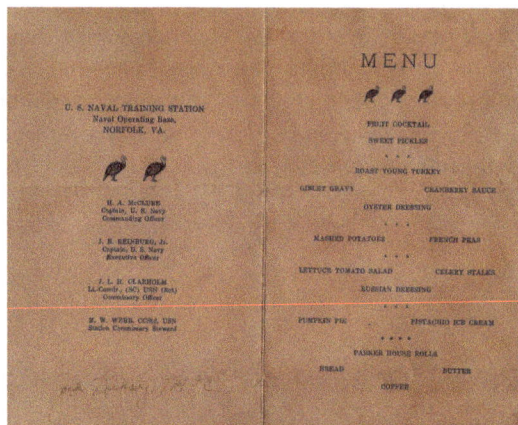

Figure 140. Original Thanksgiving Day menu from the Navy Training Station in Norfolk where Kirksey took his boot camp training. He sent this home to his wife Kloye Ann and signed it. The signature although light can be seen at bottom left. (Frank J. Andruss Sr. collection)

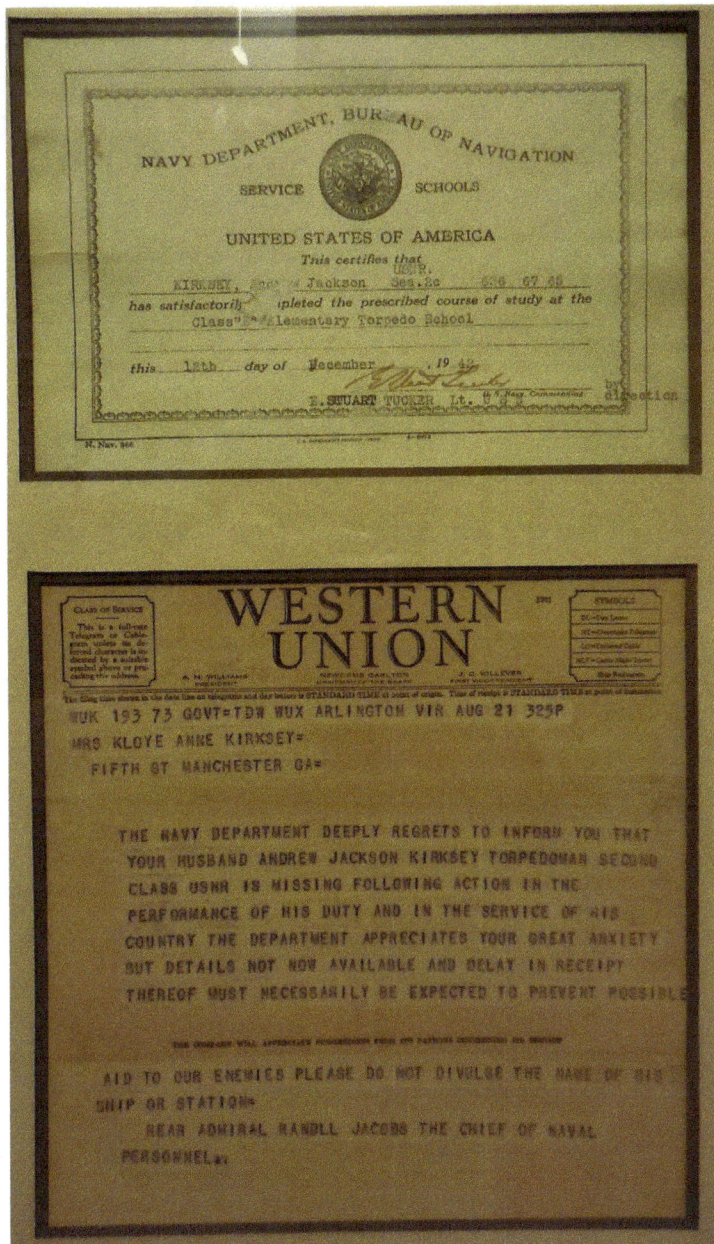

Figure 141. Kirksey artifacts include his certificate from Elementary Torpedo School (top) which he received on December 12, 1942, and a Western Union Telegram (bottom) addressed to his wife Kloye on August 21, 1943. The telegram sadly informs her that he is missing in action. (Frank J. Andruss Sr. collection)

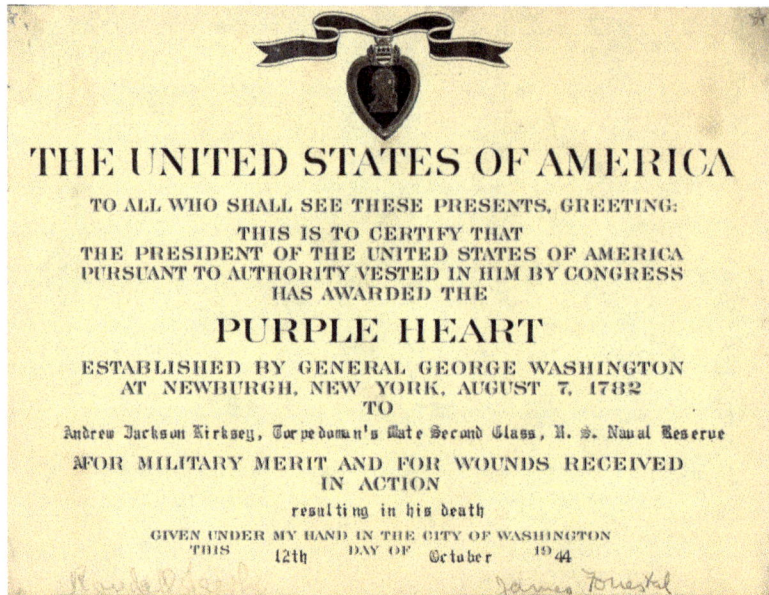

Figure 142. Navy Military Purple Heart certificate for Torpedoman's Mate Second Class Andrew Jackson Kirksey, US Naval Reserve. (Kirksey family collection)

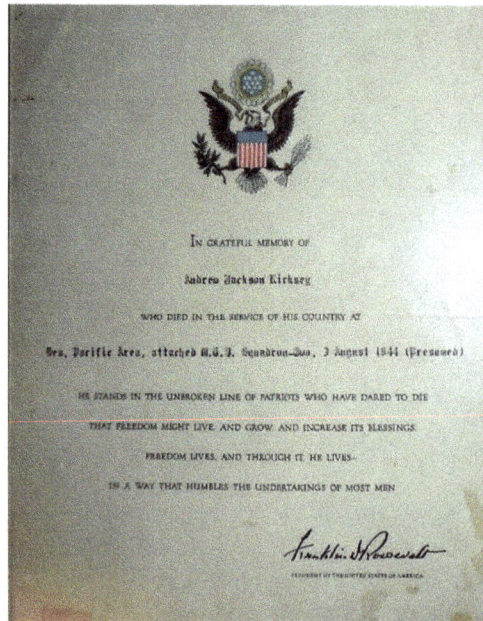

Figure 143. Presidential Purple Heart certificate for TM2/c Andrew Jackson Kirksey. (Frank J. Andruss Sr. collection)

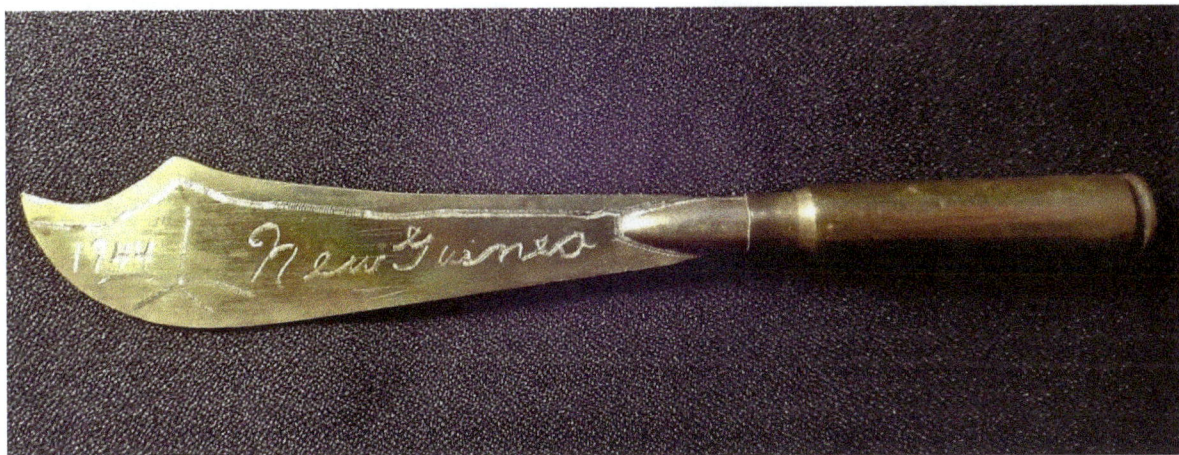

Figure 144. Knife made by the base force for GM1/c Wallace McNeish who served on PT 374 in RON 27. This was made using shell casings. (Frank J. Andruss Sr. collection)

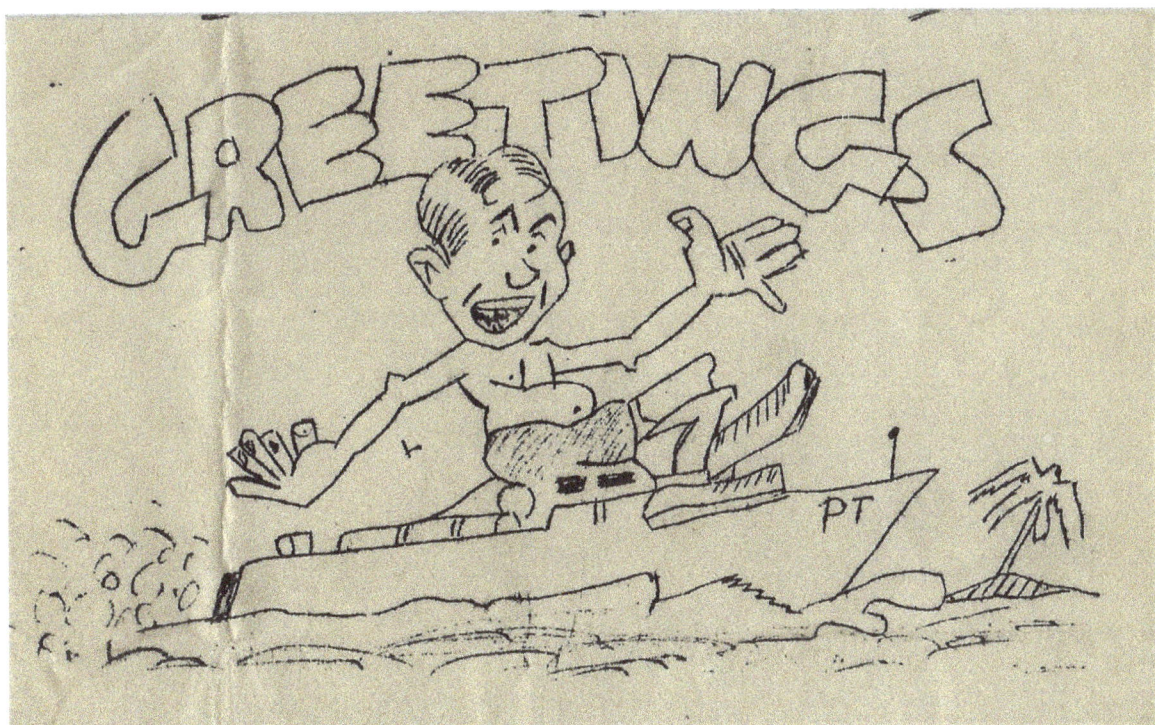

Figure 145. Greeting card brought home by Robert Bushey who would serve on PT 106 with RON 5. (Frank J. Andruss Sr. collection)

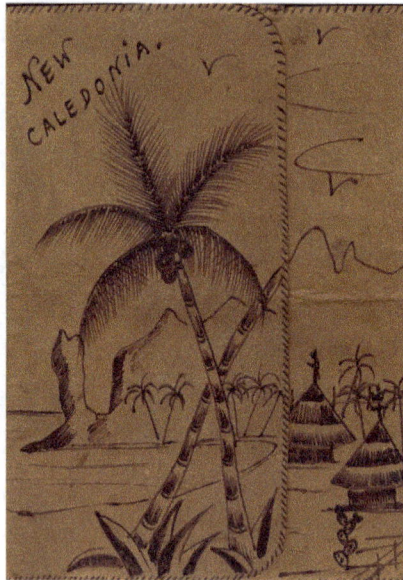

Figure 146. Binder with Island scene from New Caledonia. Taken home by GM1/c Wallace McNeish who had it aboard PT 374. Inside the binder was stationary and envelopes to write letters home. (Frank J. Andruss Sr. collection)

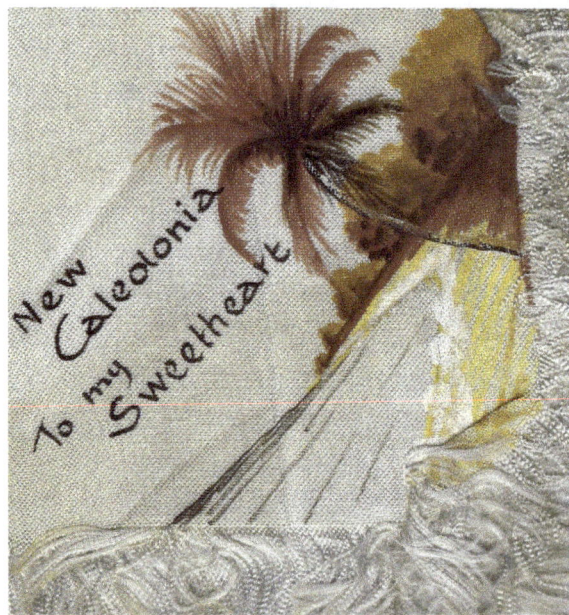

Figure 147. New Caledonia souvenir handkerchief brought home by GM1/c Wallace McNeish. (Frank J. Andruss Sr. collection)

Figure 148. It was not uncommon for a crewmen with special drawing skills to draw photos or even paint something on the boat's forward charthouse. This drawing was done by crewmen aboard PT 150 and brought home by QM3/c William E. Garfield. (Frank J. Andruss Sr. collection)

Figure 149. Here is a wooden painted model of a PT boat. This was made by Wally Kurtz who served on Base 17 in the Philippines.(Frank J. Andruss Sr. collection)

Figure 150. Wonderful Igorot carvings from Baguio in Northern Luzon, Philippines. Brought home by Dr. Alfred Skinner who was Skipper on PT 595 RON 40. (Dr. Al Skinner collection)

Figure 151. A wonderful example of a Chronometer which is a Hamilton brand (model 22). These were important to give an accurate time when using a sextant to determine one's true position. (Wally Boerger collection)

Beverly S. Kinlaw
1234 Columbus Circle
Wilmington, NC 28403
bsk7777@aol.com

August 11, 2005

Mr. Frank J. Andruss Sr.
The Mosquito Fleet Exhibit
16 Liberty Street
Feeding Hills, MA 01030

Dear Frank,

Enclosed you will find United States Navy utensils that were a part of my father's PT Boat days. As you are aware, my father, Gordon B. Kinlaw, Sr., served on PT 111 with Squadron 2. He was their Head Quartermaster and was wounded in action on February 3, 1943 when their PT Boat, commanded by Lt. John H. Clagett, was hit by enemy gunfire from a Japanese Destroyer two miles southwest of Savo Island in the Pacific.

All of the crew were rescued and among them were several who were wounded. One man later died from his wounds. My father, a Purple Heart recipient, was one of the wounded during this enemy gunfire and as a young girl I was always amazed by the scars and the fact that he still had shrapnel from these injuries in his back. My father related to me how much he enjoyed his time with PT Boats and as a proud member of the US Navy. I don't think he would have traded that experience for anything in the world.

These Navy knifes, forks and spoon were used by my father on PT 111. I hope that you can use these as part of your PT Boat Exhibit. My father would be very proud that one of his "souvenirs" would be displayed so passionately.

In closing, thank you Frank for all of your dedicated work in getting the word out on the wonderful job these PT Boat men did during the war. Your exhibit is fantastic and is in keeping with the Navy's highest standards.

Sincerely,

Rev. Beverly S. Kinlaw
Daughter of Gordon B Kinlaw, Sr.

USS PT 111
ELECTRIC BOAT COMPANY
ELCO NAVAL DIVISION
BAYONNE, N.J.
DESIGNER AND BUILDER
1942

Figure 152. Here is a letter from the daughter of QM1/c Gordon B. Kinlaw Sr. He was injured on February 3, 1943 while serving with RON 2 aboard PT 111. The artifacts he brought home played a crucial role in the daily life of every sailor, but are not thought of very much (see next page). (Frank J. Andruss Sr. collection)

Figure 153. Here are the utensils that Kinlaw brought home from PT 111. (Frank J. Andruss Sr. collection)

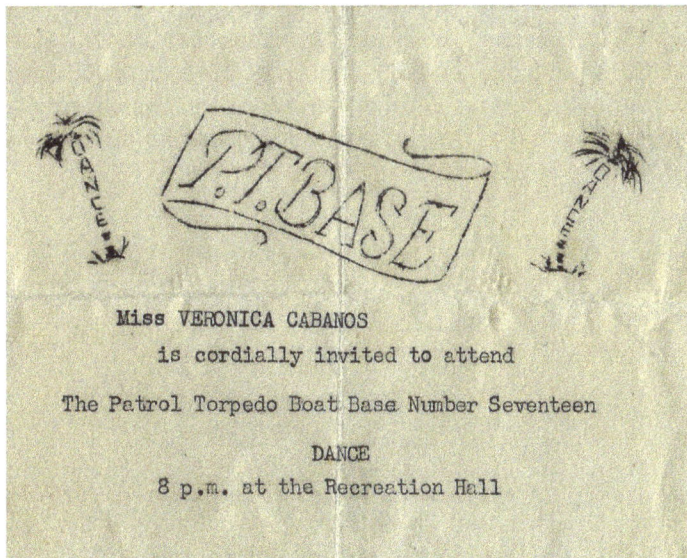

Figure 154. Invitation to Veronica Cabanos to attend a dance at the base. This is Base 17 in the Philippines, which was the largest PT boat base ever constructed during the war. (Frank J. Andruss Sr. collection)

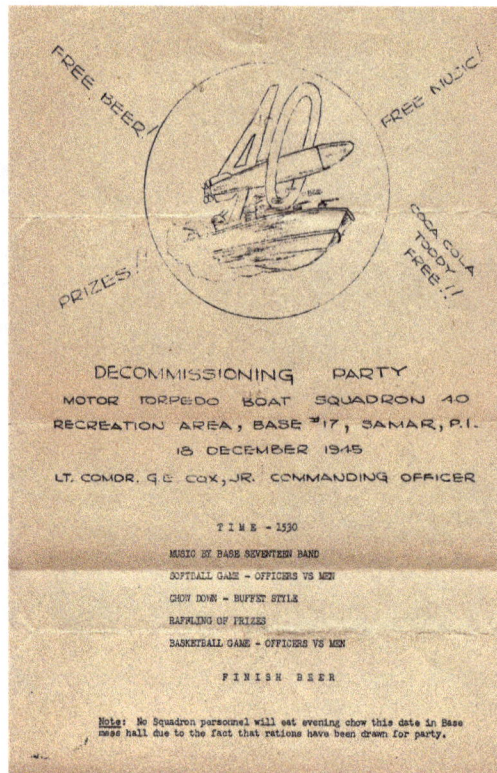

Figure 155. A decommissioning party invitation for RON 40. A Base 17 affair which took place on December 18, 1945. Plenty of things to do including the Base 17 band, raffles and beer. This was scheduled by Lt. Comdr. G. E. Cox Jr. commanding officer for RON 40. (Frank J. Andruss Sr. collection)

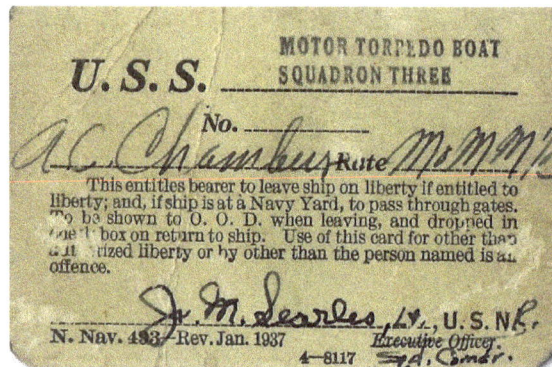

Figure 156. "Motor Torpedo Boat Squadron Three" Liberty pass for Momm1/c, A.C. Chambers and signed by Squadron commander John M. Searles. (Frank J. Andruss Sr.)

Crew of P.T. 342   Panama City
Oct. 1943

Figure 157. Sailors from PT 342 relax while in Panama City taken in October 1943. Many sailors received these as souvenirs of their time spent before heading out to the war zone. This photo was taken at a place called Cantina Tommy's. (Frank J. Andruss Sr. collection.)

Figure 158. Greeting card showing a PT boat and saying "Greetings from the Southwest Pacific." (Frank J. Andruss Sr. collection)

Figure 159. Greeting card using V-Mail for a Merry Christmas and a drawing of PT boat. Sent by A. W. Webber from the USS *Murray* (DD 576) to P.K. Hawks, a Radioman with RON 21. (Frank J. Andruss Sr. collection)

Figure 160. Original American propaganda leaflet. These were usually air dropped over occupied territory and were written in both American and Japanese. This one was an attempt to get the Japanese to surrender to American foces. Those wanting to surrender could hand this to any American officer. This was brought home by QM3/c William E. Garfield. (Frank J. Andruss Sr. collection)

Figure 161. Japanese currency, which almost all Allied sailors managed to bring home. This type of currency was issued by the Japanese Military Authority as a replacement for local currency in conquered colonies. Brought home by GM1/c Wallace McNeish of PT 374. (Frank J. Andruss Sr. collection)

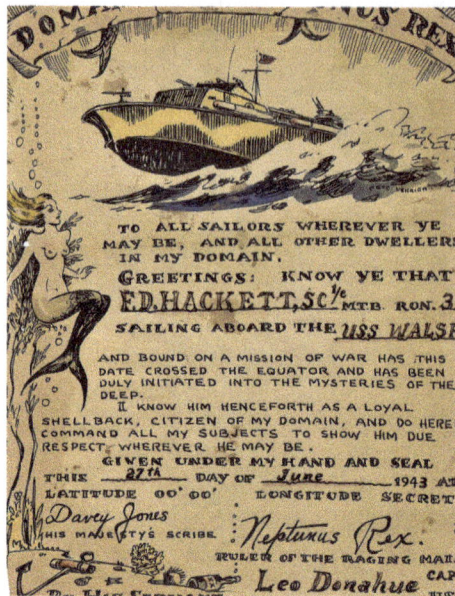

Figure 162. Equator crossing was common practice for PT sailors. Here is a Shellback certificate awarded to Sc1/c F.D.Hackett with RON 3 aboard the USS *Walsh* in 1943. (Frank J. Andruss Sr. collection)

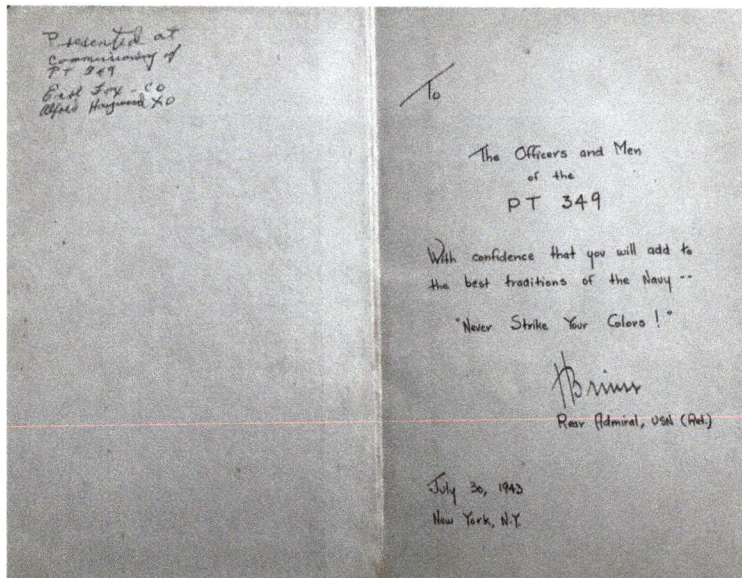

Figure 163. Watch Officer's Manual owned by CO of PT 349 Earl Fox. From 1943 this has been dedicated to officers and men of the 349. (Wally Boerger collection)

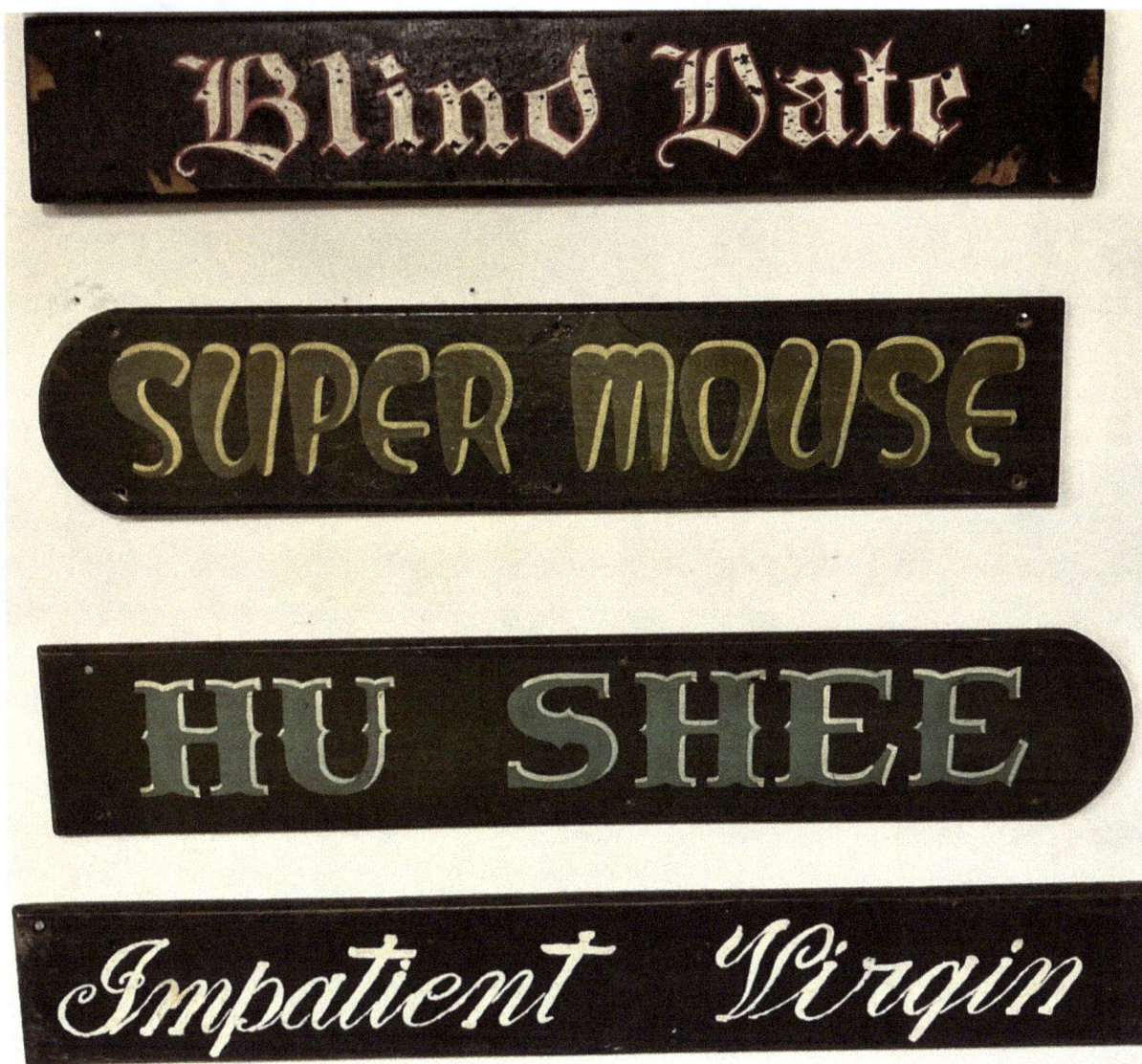

Figure 164. Wonderful preserved examples of name plates that were actually painted and tacked up onto the boats. Reminiscent of "nose art" on war-time aircraft. From the top we see. PT 494 "Blind Date", PT 589 "Super Mouse", PT 582 "Hu-Shee", and "Impatient Virgin"—two boats had this name, PT 250 and PT 492. (PT Boats Inc. collection)

KEEPING THEM IN THE PUBLIC EYE

During the dark early days of the US participation in World War II, Pearl Harbor was a disaster, and the Philippines, Guam and Wake Island were being attacked. America back home was longing for some good news. This good news was provided by the little PT boats from Motor Torpedo Boat Squadron 3. Led by their daring commander Lt. John D. Bulkeley, the PT boats helped in the defense of Bataan and Corregidor in the Philippines. Low on fuel and supplies these little boats quickly became the only Allied naval vessels remaining to resist the Japanese onslaught. News of their exploits made it back home as the "David and Goliath" myth became a reality. The PT boat quickly became the darling of the press and in this section we will take a look at many of the ways the boats made their way into popular culture (and marketing), adorning everything from comic books to candy cigarette boxes.

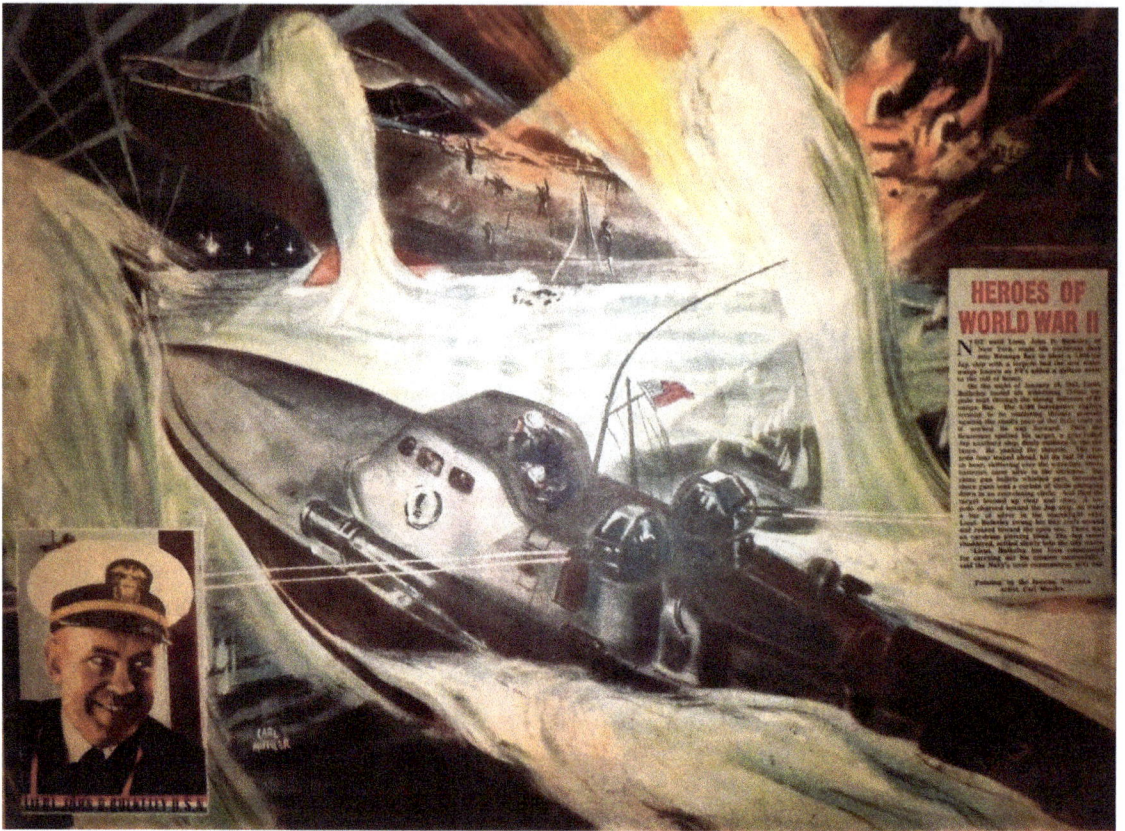

Figure 165. A very nice publication that appeared in New York newspapers as a Sunday pull-out section. The was an original painting by artist Carl Mueller depicting the exploits of Lt. John D. Bulkeley of RON 3 fame in the Philippines. It was part of the estate of Frederick Bulkeley, who was John's father. (Frank J. Andruss Sr. collection)

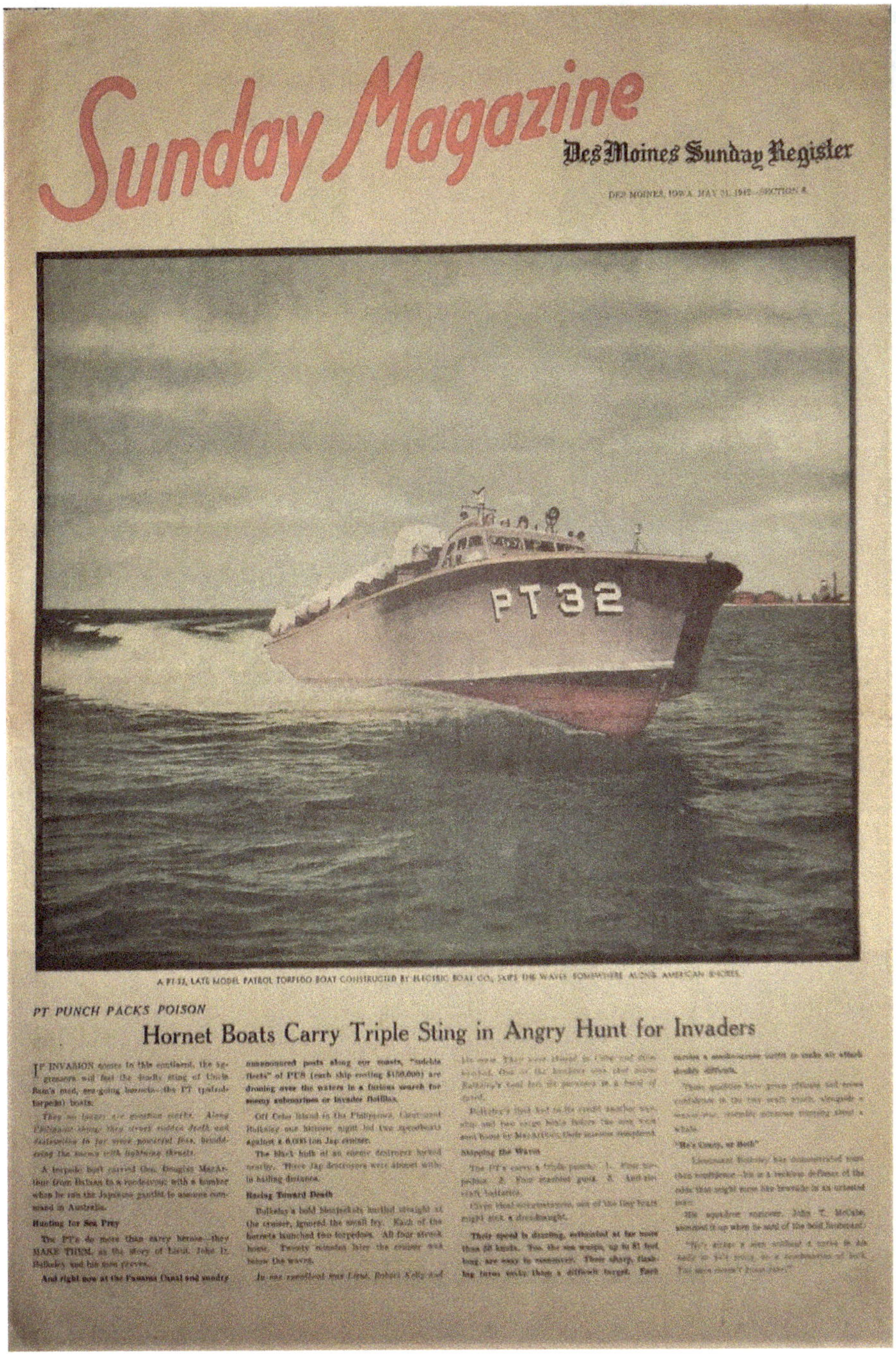

Sunday Magazine

Des Moines Sunday Register

A PT-32, LATE MODEL PATROL TORPEDO BOAT CONSTRUCTED BY ELECTRIC BOAT CO., SKIPS THE WAVES SOMEWHERE ALONG AMERICAN SHORES.

PT PUNCH PACKS POISON

Hornet Boats Carry Triple Sting in Angry Hunt for Invaders

Hunting for Sea Prey

Racing Toward Death

Skipping the Waves

Figure 166. Wonderful color pull-out section from the *Des Moines Sunday Register.* This was a part of the Frederick Bulkeley estate and shows PT 32, one of Elco's seventy-seven foot boats in RON 3. (Frank J. Andruss Sr. collection)

Figure 167. A wonderful war-time poster depicting one of the little PT boats attacking and torpedoing a Japanese warship in the Philippines. In command of PT 34 was Lt. Robert B. Kelly who took part in the operation to evacuate General Douglas MacArthur and his staff from Corregidor to Mindanao, on the night of March 12/13, 1942, and was subsequently awarded the Silver Star. (Frank J. Andruss Sr. collection)

Figure 168. Envelopes which advertised the PT boats were used throughout the war. Here we see two such examples showing the early seventy-foot Elco PT boats crashing through the waves. (Frank J. Andruss Sr. collection)

Figure 169. Two more examples of war-time envelopes that kept the PT
boats in the public eye. (Frank J. Andruss Sr. collection)

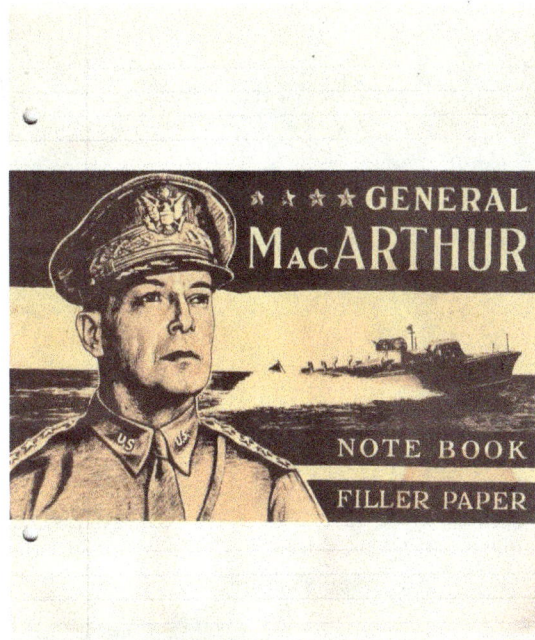

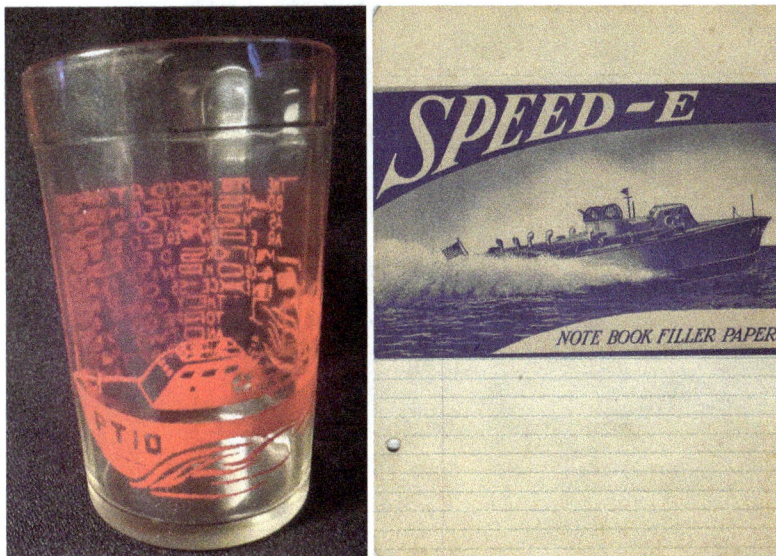

Figure 170, 171, 172. Notebook filler paper showing yellow lined paper. General Douglas MacArthur is on the paper sleeve with a PT running through the water. A fine example of a PT-themed drinking glass for the home front. On the glass is a red-colored Elco PT 10 seventy foot boat, with a description of the boat on the other side. Speed- E notebook filler paper showing a speeding PT 10 as she moves through the waves. This type of paper would appeal to younger audiences. (Frank J. Andruss Sr. collection)

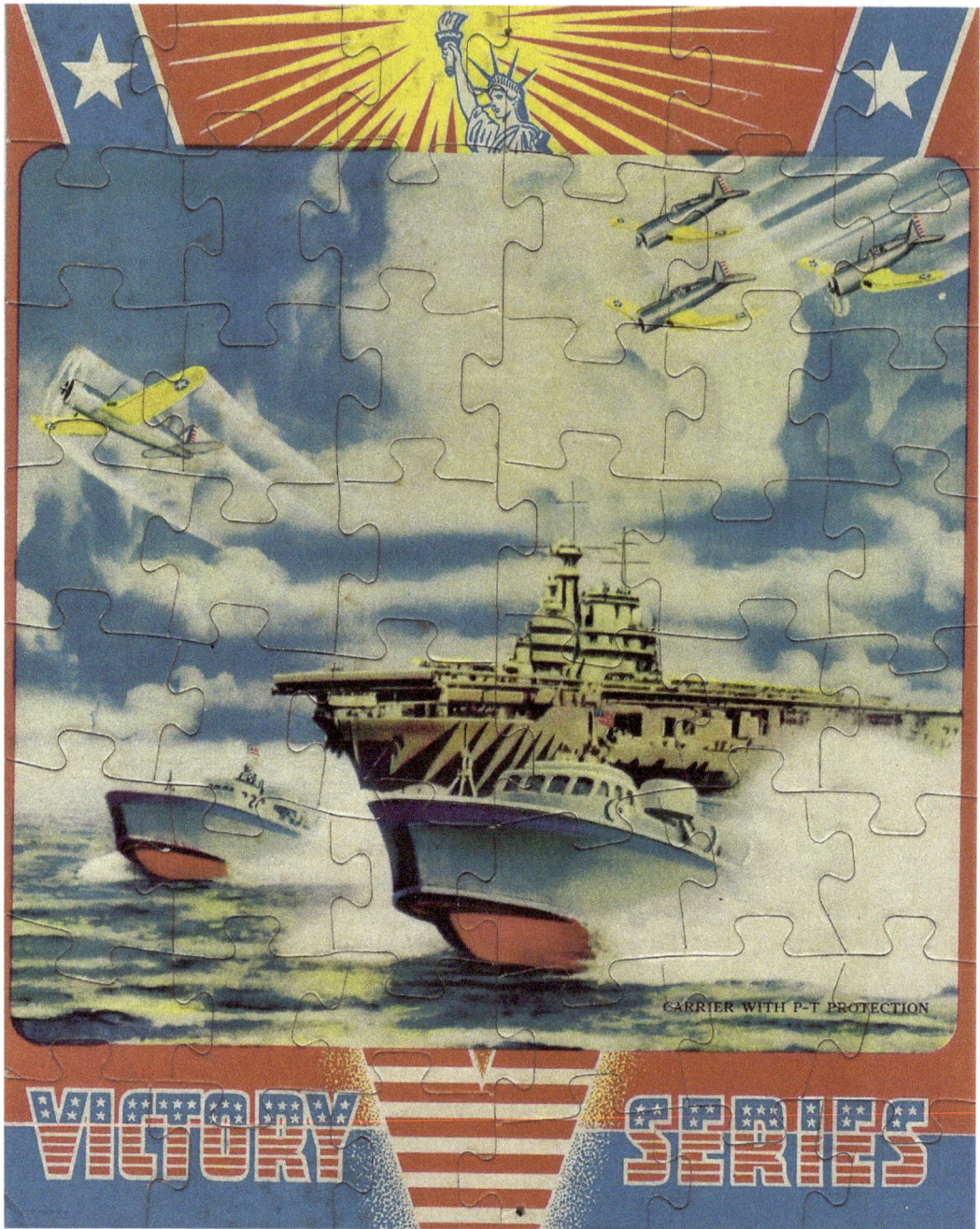

Figure 173. A pristine example of a puzzle, showing two speeding PT boats in front of an aircraft carrier. This was from the World War II Victory series. (Frank J. Andruss Sr. collection)

A PT Squadron of the U. S. Navy

NA3

Official U. S. Navy Photograph.

AS-2

Figure 174. Postcards were a popular way to send greeitngs to loved ones. These examples show PT squadrons in action together. (Frank J. Andruss Sr. collection)

Figure 175. One of the more colorful postcards that was available during World War II reads "U.S.N. Carrier with P-T Protection" While this was not a realistic scenario (PTs never operated as carrier escorts) and the punctuation is imaginative, the spirit is strong. (Frank J. Andruss Sr. collection)

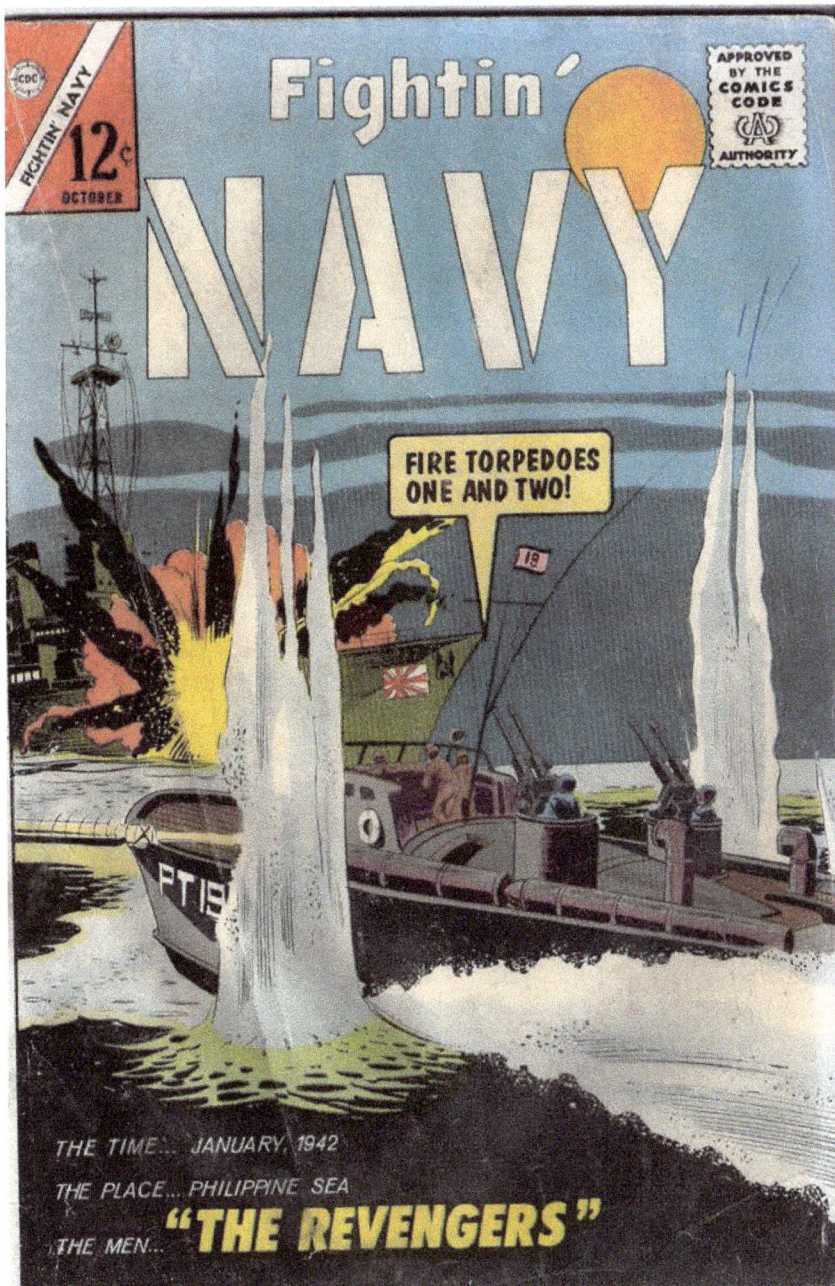

Figure 176. Children's comic books during the war years were very popular and beyond into the 50's and 60's. Here we see PT boats striking back at the enemy. (Frank J. Andruss Sr. collection)

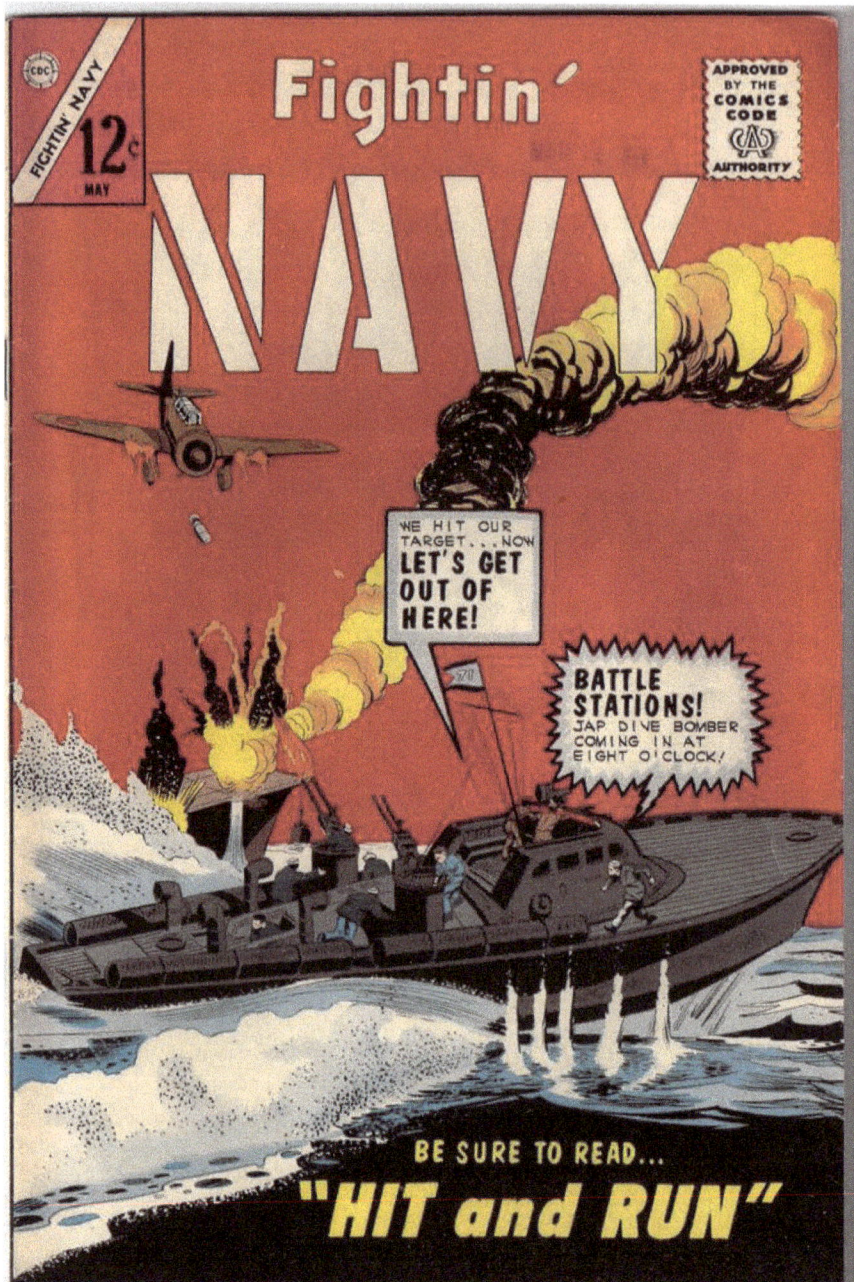

Figure 177. This children's comic illustrates the logic of the "hit and run" warfare that was appropriate to the early period of the war. (Frank J. Andruss Sr. collection)

Figure 178. Even calendars from the period used PT boats as their main theme. Here we see two young boys constructing a model, while they dream of the boat running through the waves. This calendar is from a restaurant called Pete's Place and is dated 1945. (Frank J. Andruss Sr. collection)

Figure 179. Nothing better on Christmas than to have a tie just like Dad's. This pristine example, still in its box and never opened, shows a PT on the lower part of the tie. (Frank J. Andruss Sr. collection)

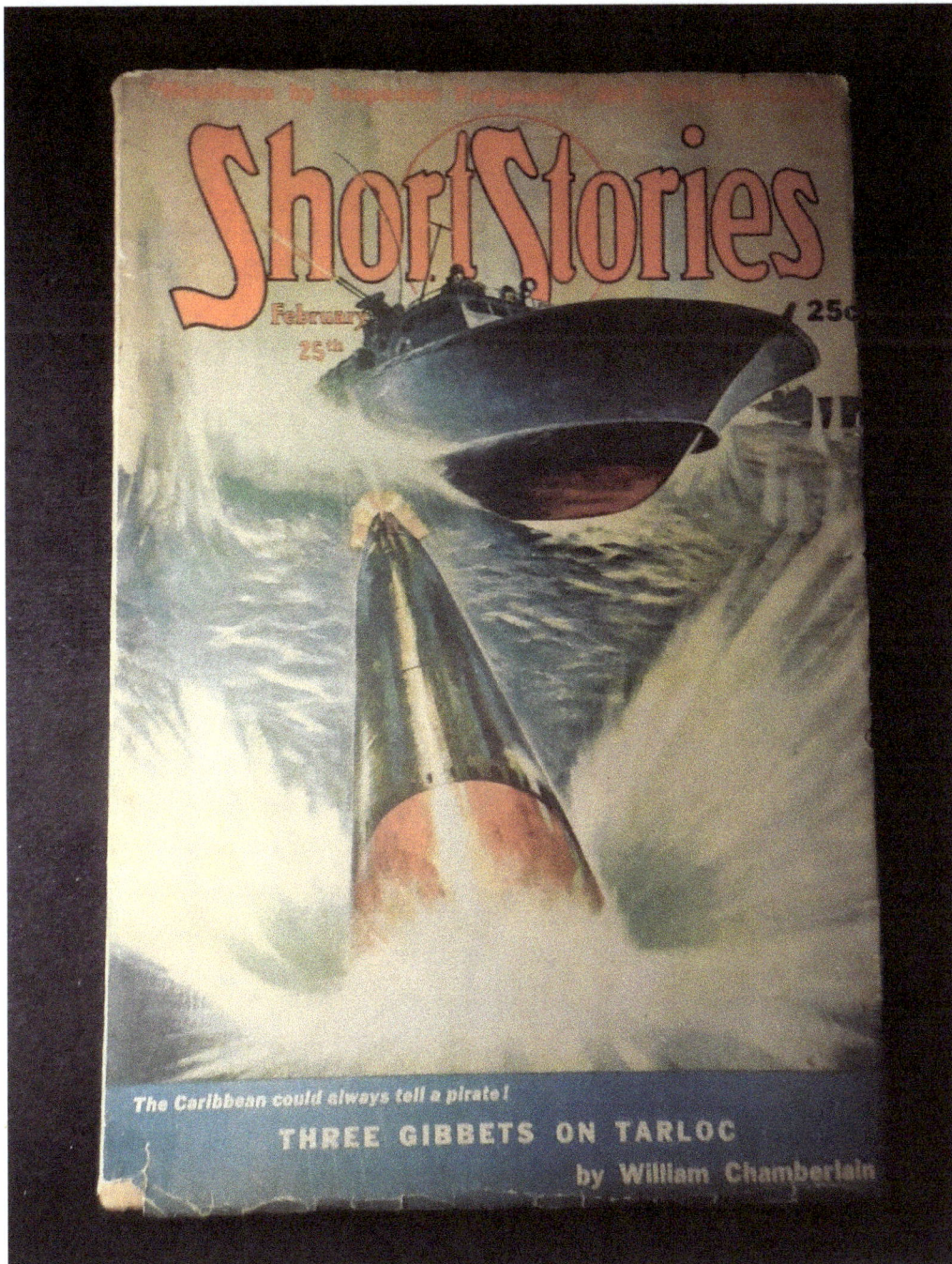

Figure 180. Books and magazines also used the PT boats on their covers. This cover art by Edgar Franklin Wittmack for *Short Stories* (v. 186 #4, #916, February 25th, 1944) shows a PT boat firing a torpedo at the enemy. (Frank J. Andruss Sr. collection)

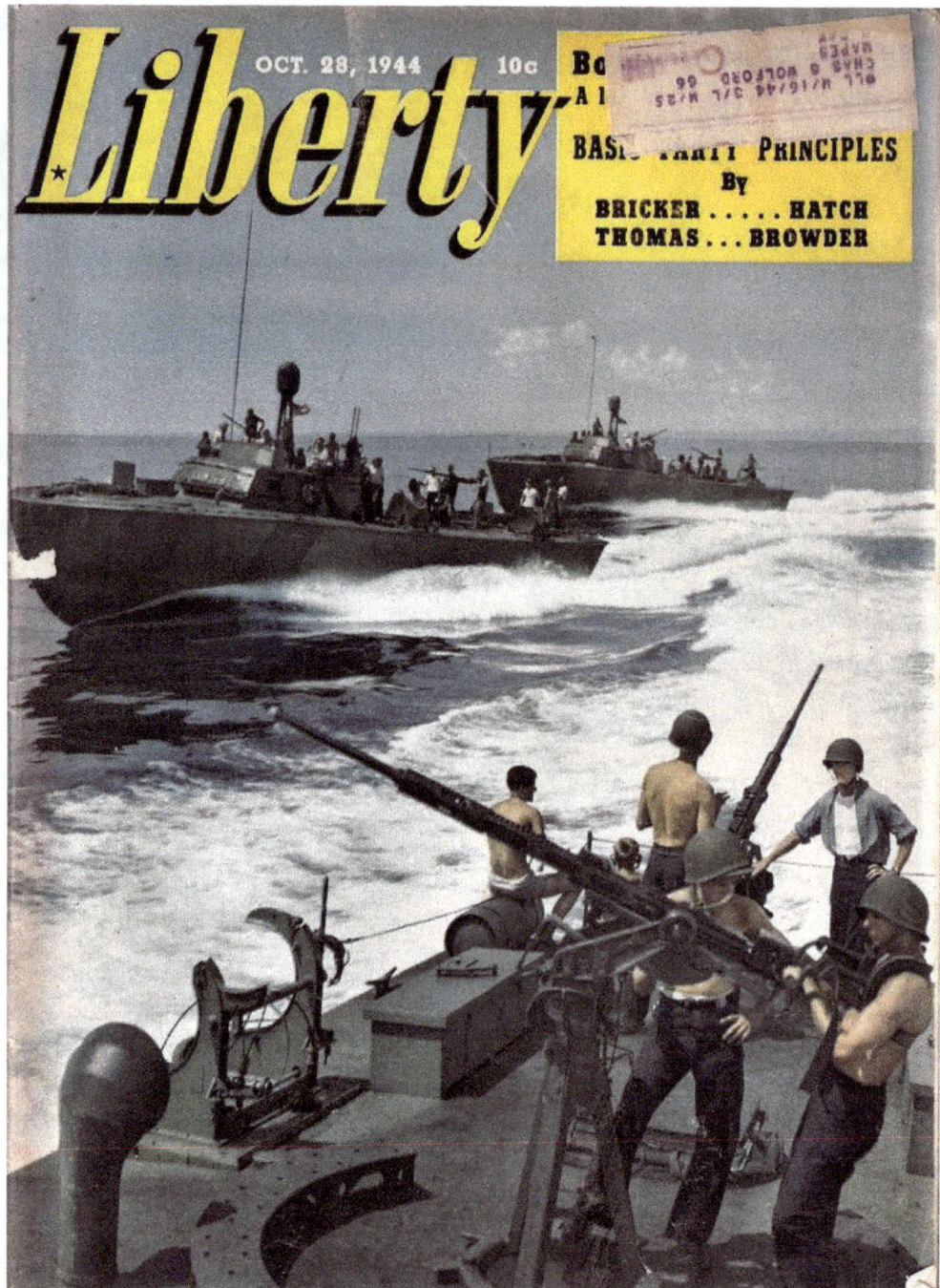

Figure 181. A *Liberty* magazine from 1944 showing Higgins PT boats while in Panama. (Frank J. Andruss Sr. collection)

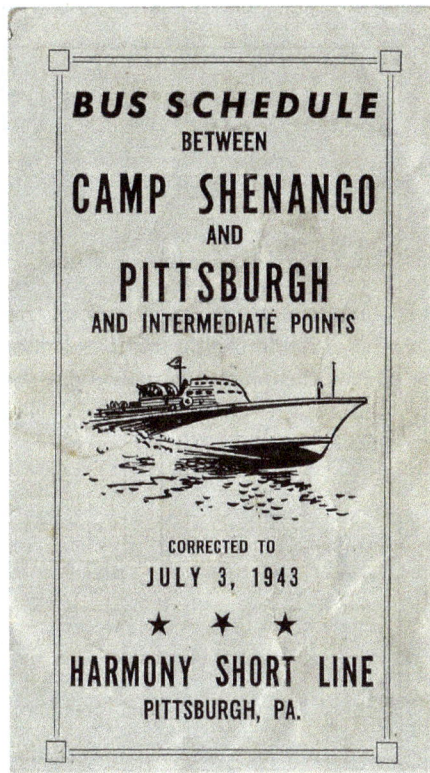

Figure 182. The Harmony Short Line in Pittsburgh used a PT Boat on the cover of its schedule in 1943. (Frank J. Andruss Sr. collection)

Figure 183. Even a student bus pass from the St. Louis Public Service Company used the "Mosquito Boat" from "Uncle Sam's Navy" as its subject matter, this one in 1942. (Frank J. Andruss Sr. collection)

Figure 184. The PT boat was used on the back of this Raleigh candy cigarette box. This was one of thirty different photos used during the war. The boat in this photo was claimed as "A mile a minute midget boat" and depicts PT 17, one of Elco's seventy-footers. (Frank J. Andruss Sr. collection)

Figure 185. The Veribrite Factory in Chicago used the PT boats in its advertisements for licorice lozenges. This box shows PT 311 on the cover with a five cent cost per box. (Frank J. Andruss Sr. collection)

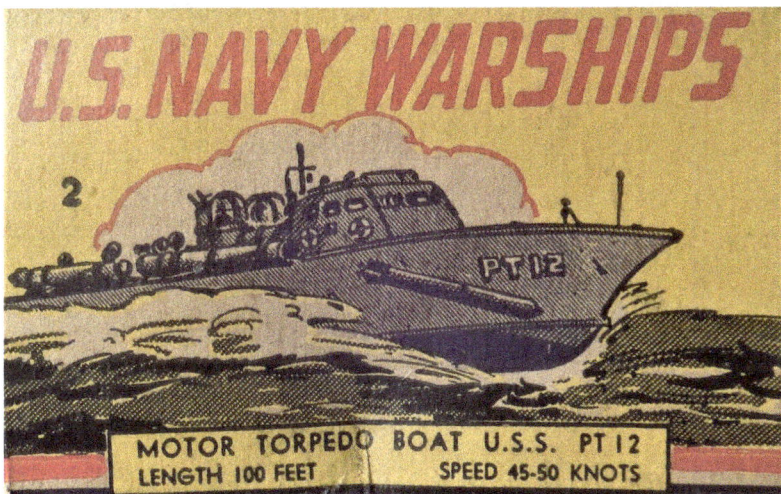

Figure 186. This item from the "US Navy Warships" series of candy boxes from Novel Packaging Corporation shows PT 12 as she zips though the ocean and releases a torpedo (American Card Catalog R98, http://www.non-sport.com/sets/r98.php). A very colorful box although the claimed length of 100 feet was inaccurate as PT 12 was a seventy-foot Elco boat. The claim that the boat could do fifty knots, seen in many advertisements in the era, was alsot false. (Frank J. Andruss Sr. collection)

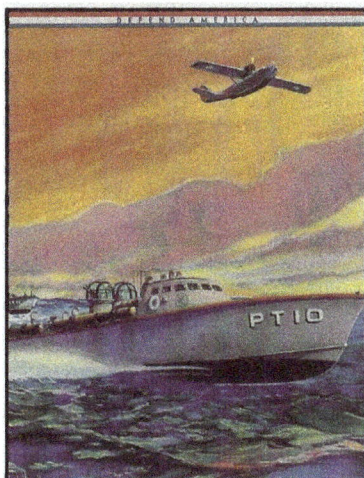

Figure 187. A beautiful small poster of Victory as part of the Defend America series. This card—as colorful as it gets—depicts Elco's first assembled PT 10 as she makes her way across the waves accompanied by a single-engined flying boat. (Frank J. Andruss Sr. collection)

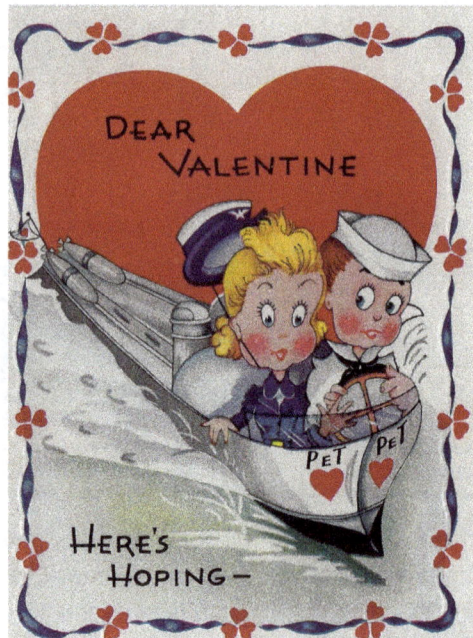

Figure 188. Even war-time Valentine cards got into the action by using PT boats as a sweetheart theme. This card shows a sailor with his girl as they bounce across the sea. (Frank J. Andruss Sr. collection)

Figure 189. The inside of the above card shows the little PT voat torpedo an enemy ship and makes a "big hit" with his girl. (Frank J. Andruss Sr. collection)

Figure 190. This war-time valentine card shows the cute little sailor girl as she scouts for a valentine just like you. (Frank J. Andruss Sr. collection)

Figure 191. Kinney Shoes was the largest family chain shoe retailer in the United States at the beginning of 1936, with 335 stores operating nationwide. Here they have used the little PT Boat in their advertisement campaign during 1941. These cards were handed out at all stores during the war. (Frank J. Andruss Sr. collection)

Figure 192. Another giveaway card, this one from the Amoskeag National Bank in Manchester, New Hampshire. This card lets the customer know that they can buy war bonds at their bank. (Frank J. Andruss Sr. collection)

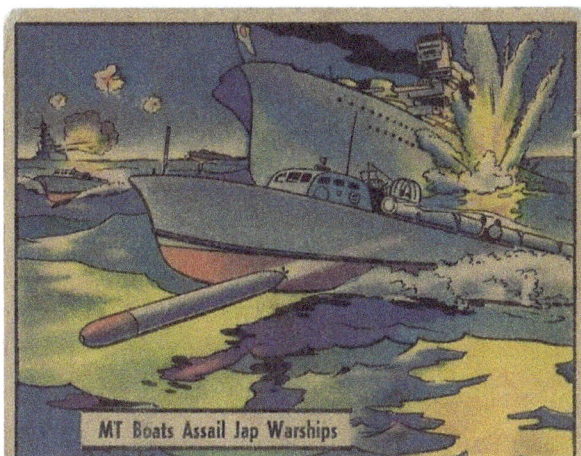

Figure 193. Bowman Gum Company used various topics as their subject matter for their children's chewing gum packages. Here is an "MT" boat using a torpedo to assail a Japanese warship. (Frank J. Andruss Sr. collection)

Figure 194. Another Bowman gum card showing a little PT boat up against a large Japanese ship. Note that these cards were only produced through 1941 as paper rations during the war stalled production. (Frank J. Andruss Sr. collection)

Figure 195. Hundreds of thousands of what some now refer to as "propaganda matchbooks" came out during the war. Here are two examples using PT boats as the subject matter, one showing the Mosquito Fleet, and the other the MTBSTC. (Frank J. Andruss Sr. collection)

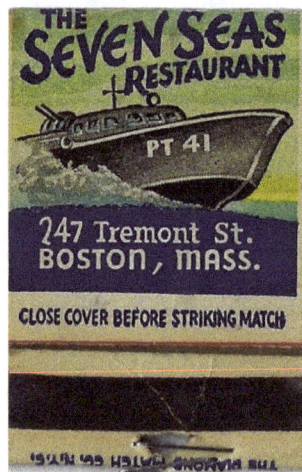

Figure 196. Another great example of a propaganda matchbook cover, only this time using one of the RON 3 PT Boats. The Seven Seas Restaurant in Boston, Massachusetts features PT 41, Lt. John D. Bulkeley's flagship while in the Philippines. (Frank J. Andruss Sr. collection)

Figure 197. One of the all time great movies involving PT boats was the 1945 classic *They Were Expendable.* With a star studded cast including Robert Montgomery, John Wayne, and Donna Reed, audiences were treated to the exploits of Motor Torpedo Boat Squadron 3 in the Philippines. This colorful ad for the movie is a rare pull-out edition. (Frank J. Andruss Sr. collection)

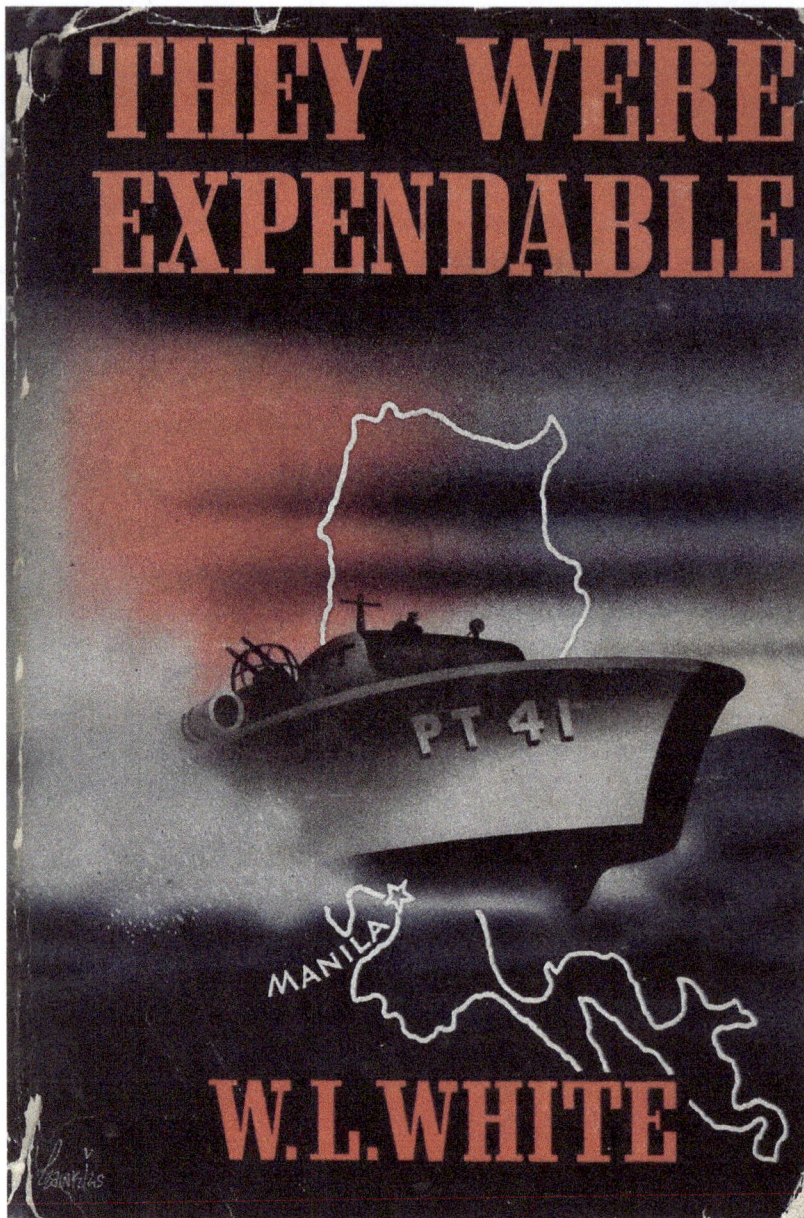

Figure 198. The book *They Were Expendable* by W. L. White was available to the public in 1942. This book was part of the library of Henry R. Sutphen who was the Executive Vice President of Elco. According to his family he had both Lt. John D. Bulkeley and Lt. Robert B. Kelly sign the book when they returned from the Philippines. Bulkeley commanded RON 3 at Cavite in the Philippines while Kelly was his executive officer. (Frank J. Andruss Sr. collection)

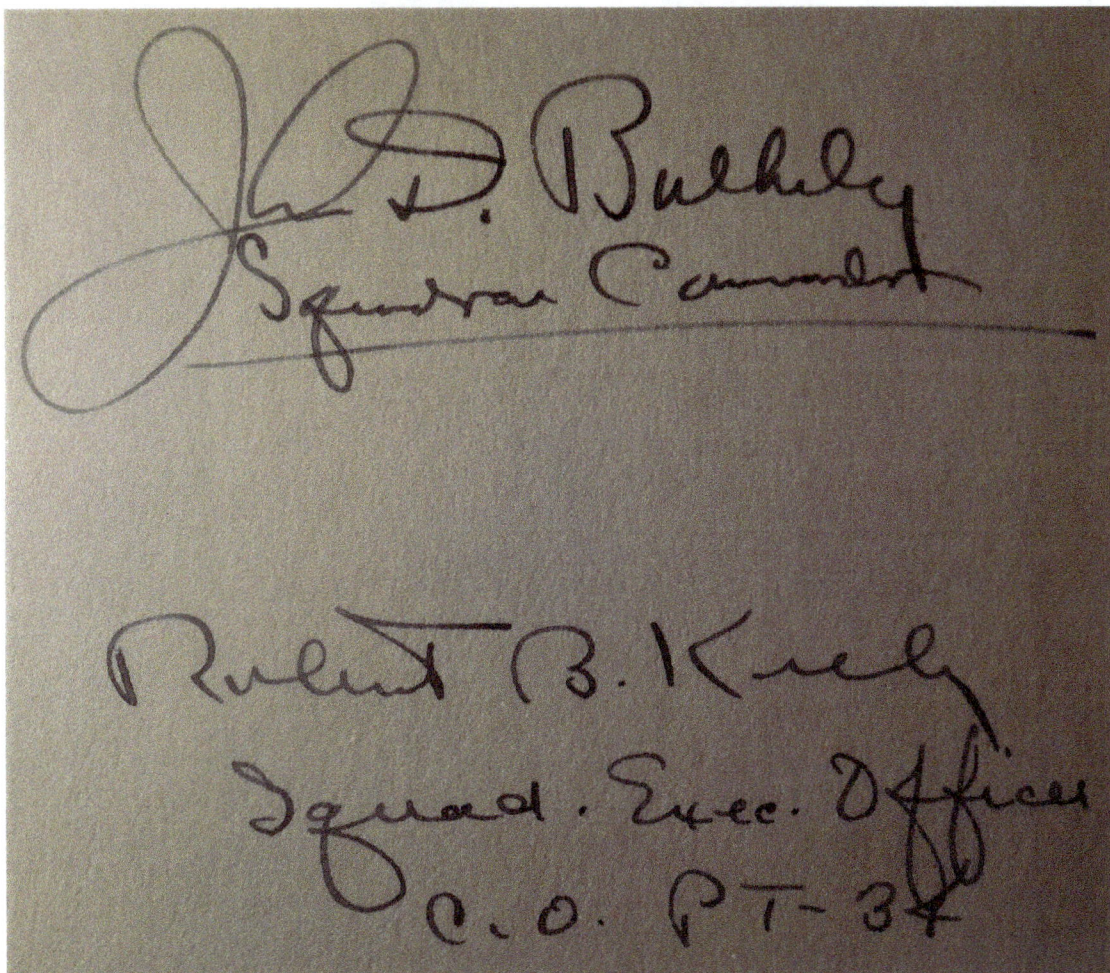

Figure 199. Inside cover of Henry Sutphen's copy of *They Were Expendable* which shows the inscription by both Bulkeley and Kelly. (Frank J. Andruss Sr. collection)

Figure 200. There is no doubt that the 1963 Warner Brother's movie *PT 109* catapulted the PT boat to the forefront of popularity. The movie depicted the actions of Lt. (j.g.) John F. Kennedy and his crew while serving in the South Pacific. For those of us old enough to remember this movie, it gave us insight into the life of Kennedy before he became our 35th President of the United States. Kennedy's war-time exploits rocket-boosted his political career. Much was made of Kennedy's genuine heroism and it did not take long before merchandise began popping up across the country. In this photo we see some of that political merchandise. (Frank J. Andruss Sr. collection)

Figure 201. Another look at political merchandise from the Kennedy era. Here we see everything from pins and matchbooks, to bracelets and contribution card depicting PT 109 on the front. (Frank J. Andruss Sr. collection)

Figure 202. Even some pencil boxes for children depicted the little PT Boats on the cover. Here are two surviving examples of those boxes. (Frank J. Andruss Sr. collection)

Figure 203. A look at the inside of one of the pencil boxes show surviving lead pencils and a ruler. (Frank J. Andruss Sr. collection)

Figure 204. Koppitz-Melchers Inc. Brewery opened in Detroit in 1934 and closed in 1947. Here is one of their unopened bottles of beer which features the little PT boats as part of their Victory Beers. (Frank J. Andruss Sr. collection)

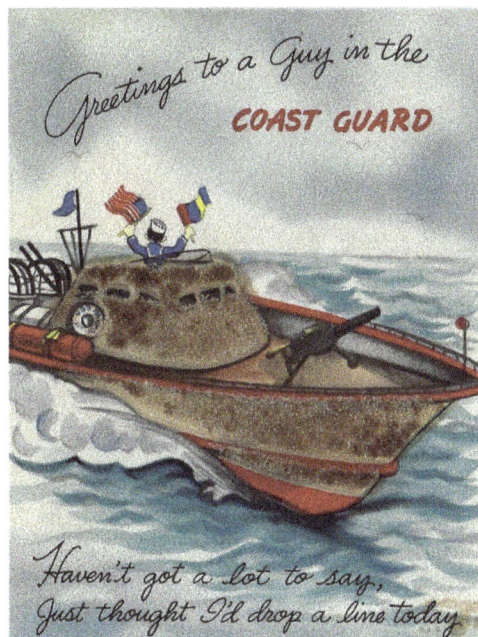

Figure 205. Although the Coast Guard during the war did not use PT boats, this beautiful greeting card shows a PT boat with "Greetings to a Guy in the Coast Guard." (Frank J. Andruss Sr. collection)

Figure 206. Here is a nice box of an Elco eighty-foot PT boat that was made by the Varney Company. Made from wood with some metal parts, glue and instruction sheet, it made a very nice model for its day. These were put out in late 1944-45. (Frank J. Andruss Sr. collection)

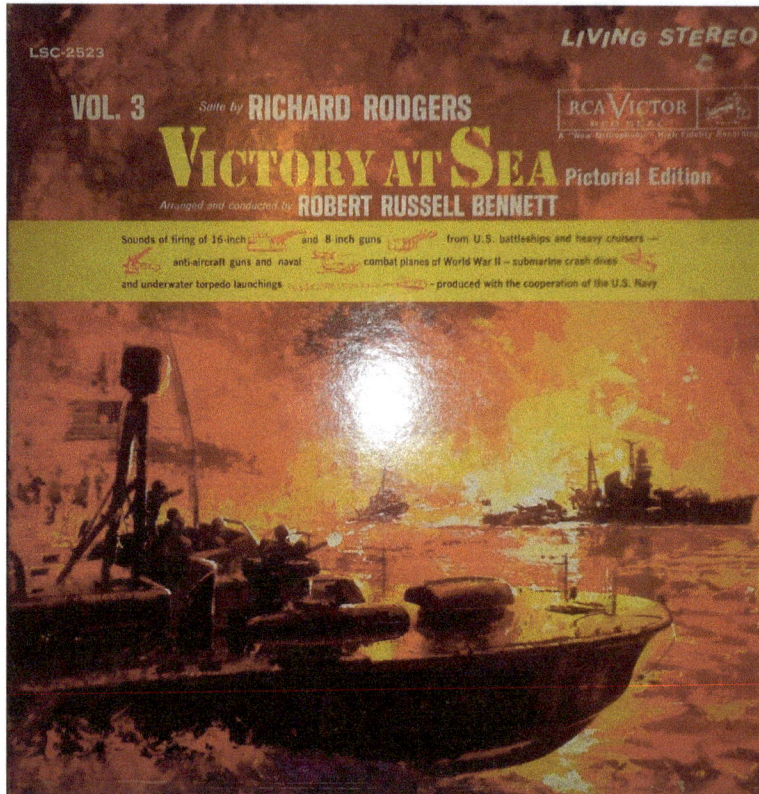

Figure 207. Here is a fine example of a *Victory at Sea* vinyl record which came out in 1961. This very popular series ran from 1952-1953, but would come back strong in the 60's. This two-record set features a night time run by a PT against an enemy ship. (Frank J. Andruss Sr. collection)

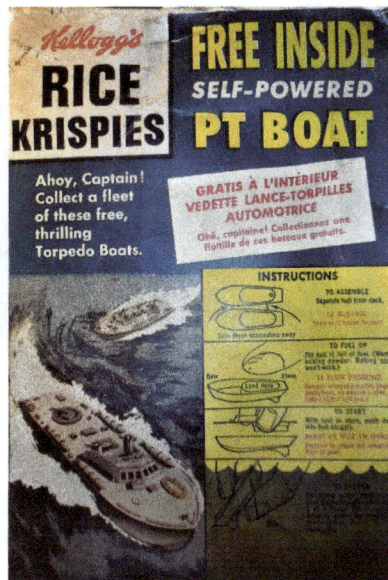

Figure 208. A fine example of keeping the PT boats in the public eye was this box of Kellogg's Rice Krispies, complete with a self-powered PT boat inside the box. This box was distributed in France. (Frank J. Andruss Sr. collection)

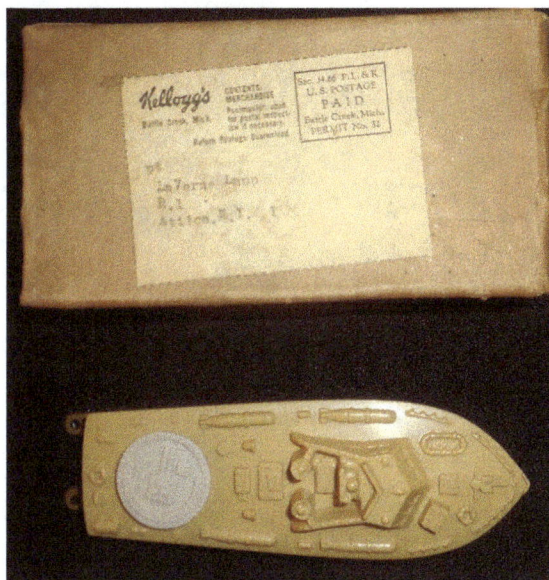

Figure 209. You could even get a larger self propelled PT Boat by writing to the Kellogg's Company. Here is a fine example complete with the shipping box. (Frank J. Andruss Sr. collection)

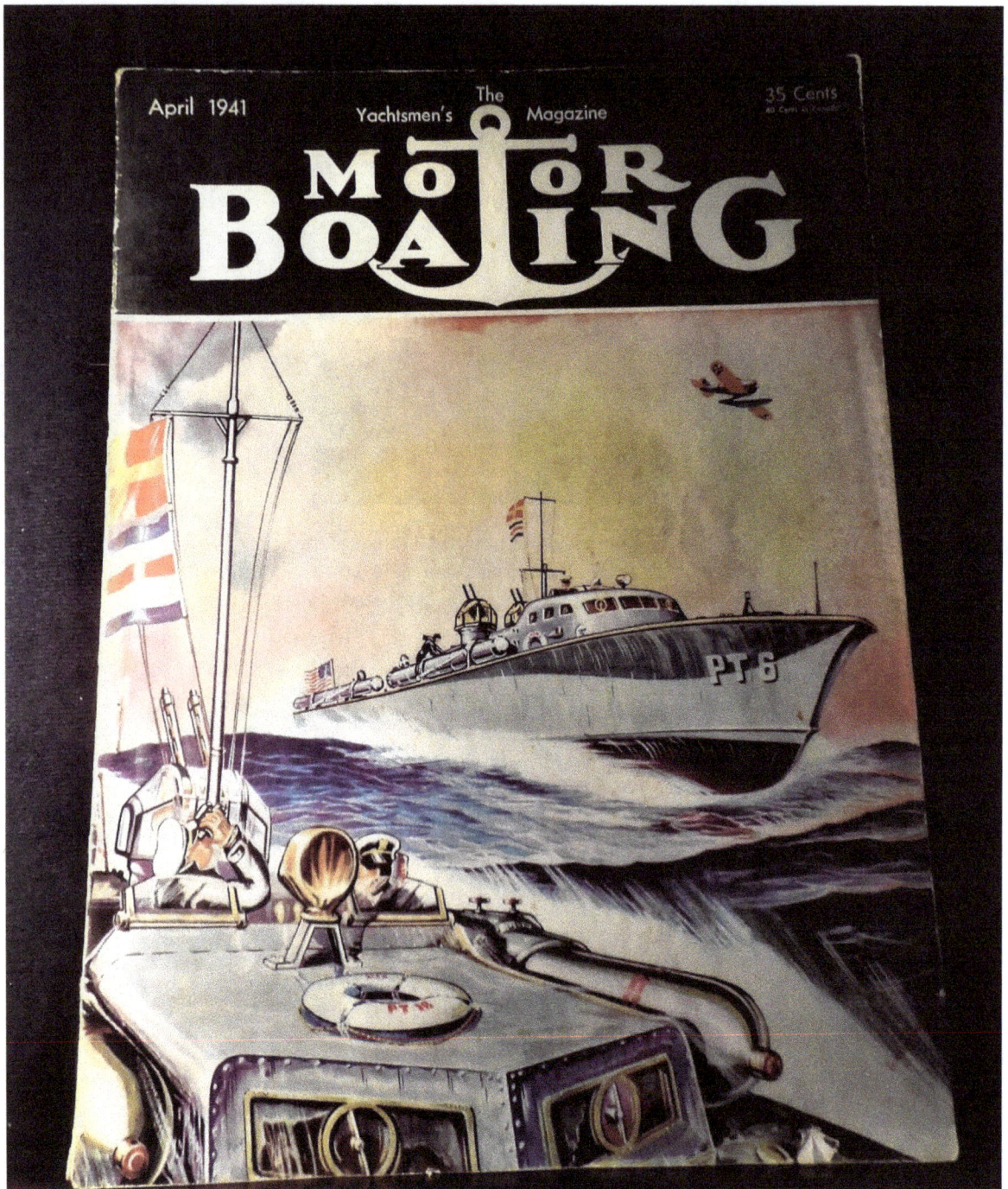

Figure 210. As mentioned before, books and magazines constantly used the PT boats as their subject matter as can be seen in this 1941 publication of *Motor Boating*. (Frank J. Andruss Sr. collection)

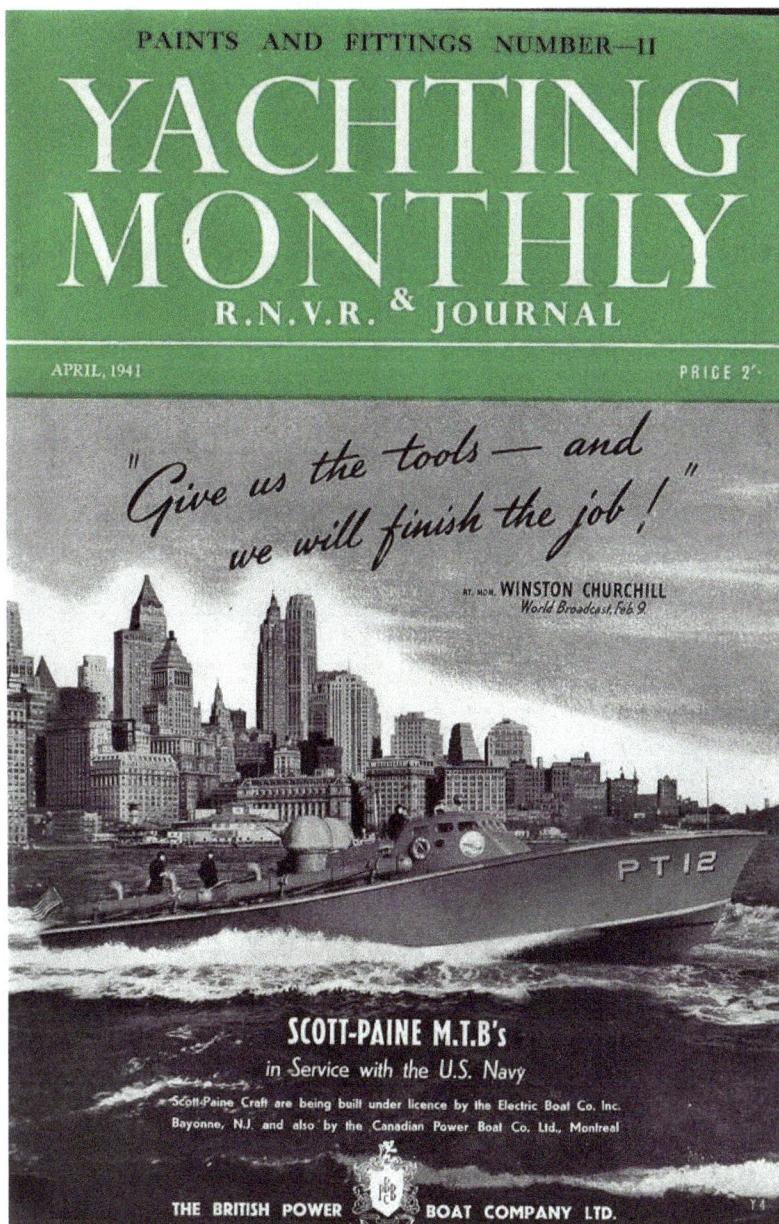

PAINTS AND FITTINGS NUMBER—II

YACHTING MONTHLY

R.N.V.R. & JOURNAL

APRIL, 1941   PRICE 2'-

"Give us the tools — and we will finish the job!"

RT. HON. WINSTON CHURCHILL
World Broadcast, Feb. 9.

PT 12

SCOTT-PAINE M.T.B's
in Service with the U.S. Navy

Scott-Paine Craft are being built under licence by the Electric Boat Co. Inc.
Bayonne, N.J. and also by the Canadian Power Boat Co. Ltd., Montreal

THE BRITISH POWER BOAT COMPANY LTD.

Figure 211. Another magazine this time from across the ocean. This *Yachting Monthly* from 1941 was a British publication but they are using one of the Elco Naval Division's seventy-footers, designated PT 12, in New York. Remember it was the Scott-Paine PT 9 that Elco bought and delivered back home as a prototype for their first assembled boats. (Frank J. Andruss Sr. collection)

Figure 212. Children could even get a PT boat tattoo as part of an insert for Cracker Jack, this one showing a color Elco boat firing at the enemy. (Frank J. Andruss Sr. collection)

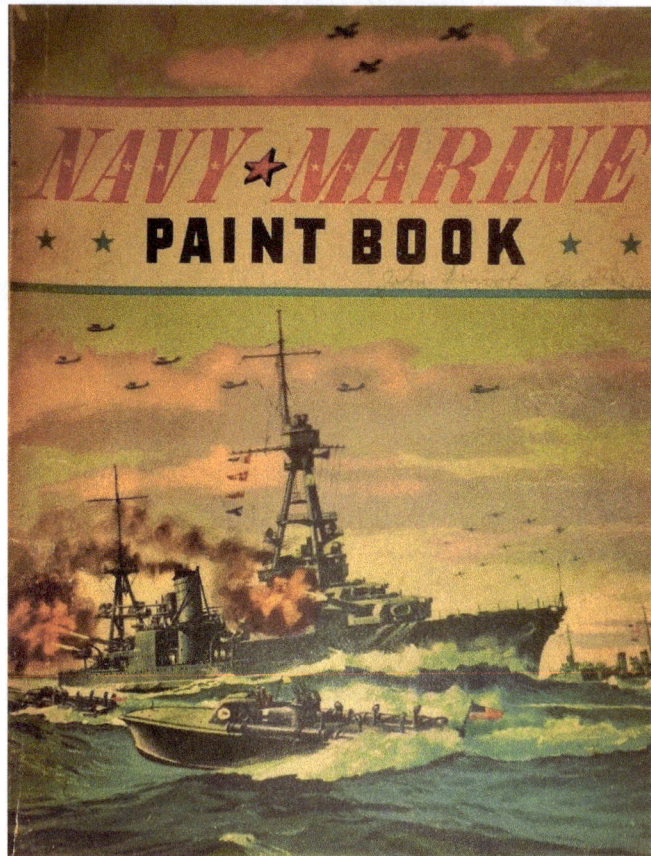

Figure 213. Here we see a Navy/Marine children's paint book with the little PT Boat right in the thick of things. (Frank J. Andruss Sr. collection)

Figure 214. Many wonderful paintings of the PT boats were done with some being sold in public markets. Even today artists use the wonderful lines of the boats in many of their subject paintings as can be seen here in this wonderful oil painting of "Knights of the Sea". (Frank J. Andruss Sr. collection)

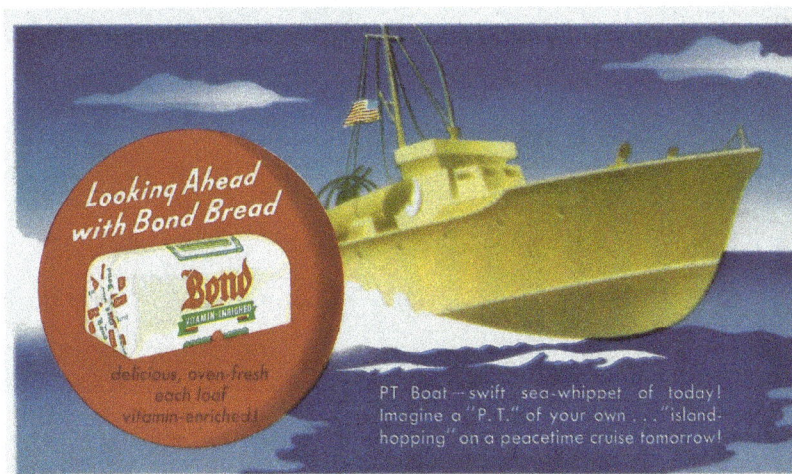

Figure 215. Even Bond Bread got into the act by using the little PT boat on their cards. "Imagine a P.T. of your own ... 'island hopping' on a peacetime cruise tomorrow."

Figure 216. Lt. Raymond P. Shafer served as CO of PT 359 and XO of PT 375 with RON 27. He earned the Bronze Star for his actions and after the war become an attorney, and in 1967, Governor of Pennsylvania. This comical framed piece is a wonderful drawing of Shafer riding PT 359 during his time as Governor. It is signed to a former crewman by Shafer. (Frank J. Andruss Sr. collection)

Figure 217. When the US entered World War Two, Little Orphan Annie not only played her part by blowing up a German submarine but organized and led groups of children called the Junior Commandos in the collection of newspapers, scrap metal, and other recyclable materials for the war effort. This 1942 sweat shirt shows Annie's commandos being dropped off by PT boats. (Frank J. Andruss Sr. collection)

UNIFORMS, JACKETS, PATCHES AND PINS

Enlisted man's clothing usually consisted of the work uniform, dungarees and shirt, the Navy blue dress uniform for winter and the white jumper for the summer months. PT boat officers usually wore the basic khaki, and dress whites. In 1943 the gray uniforms for officers arrived on the scene.

PT boaters felt the need to have a special insignia because their training was indeed specialized, similar to that of the submarine and aviation branches, but their requests fell on deaf ears until sometime in August 1943 when the Navy allowed the block letters "PT." Enlisted men serving on the boats could wear this mark on the left sleeve of both of their blue and white uniforms. It should be noted here that the PT boaters were already wearing the Walt Disney Mosquito Fleet emblem, although it was not approved at that time. Most of the PT boaters wearing this patch acquired them in the early days of Squadrons 1 and 2, during the shakedown cruises of 1941. A shoulder patch was approved in September of 1944 to replace the blocked letters.

The PT boat insignia was only authorized for enlisted men. PT boat officers usually wore the basic khaki or in 1943 the gray uniforms. The cold weather clothing for both enlisted men and officers usually consisted of the N-1 blue foul jacket and other variable underway gear to try and keep dry and warm.

PT boat pins were usually handed out by boat builders as new squadrons were being commissioned. They were also available in the ship's store at the MTBSTC. Both pin backs and tie clasps were available. Winfield J. Koch, who was stationed at Melville, came up with the idea. He drew up some designs and one of the boys at base had a father who owned a jewelry store in Attleboro, Massachusetts. The pins were soon available in silver- and gold-plated versions. It should be noted however that the pins were not authorized to be worn with the uniform, except when they could be used as tie clips for the officers and chiefs. Silver pins were usually for the enlisted men, while the gold-plated were for the officers, although both could be obtained.

Figure 218. A well-preserved example of the typical enlisted man's dress blue uniform. This uniform shows the typical Mosquito Fleet emblem on the shoulder along with Rank. Notice the gold "ruptured duck" on the breast pocket,which was actually called the Honorable Service Lapel Button or the Honorable Service Lapel Pin. It was awarded to those who were honorably discharged from service. This uniform top belonged to MoMM 2/c Kenneth Morris who served on PT 364 with RON 18. (Save the PT Boat, Inc. collection)

Figure 219. This enlisted man's dress blue uniform belonged to MoMM 3/c Maurice Hooper who served PT 238 with RON 18. Maurice served at Mindoro in the Philippines. (Save the PT Boat, Inc. collection)

Figure 220. Very nice example of an officers dress blue jacket. This belonged to Chief Radioman Pphaen Sayre who was attached to MTB base 16 in Zamboanga in the Philippines. (Save the PT Boat, Inc. collection)

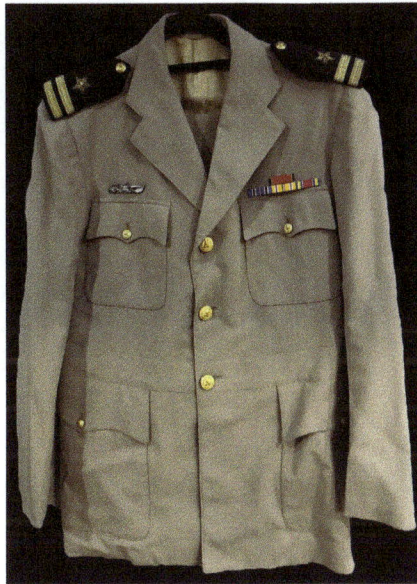

Figure 221. A typical Navy officer's uniform in the summer khaki tan color. This uniform belonged to Lt. Clement D. Blakney who was the XO on PT 257. This coat has his medals on the right, just above the pocket flap, as well as the sterling silver PT pin on the left. (Save the PT Boat, Inc. collection)

Figure 222. Khaki Officers overseas cap and Visor cap belonging to Lt. Clement D. Blakney. (Save the PT Boat, Inc. collection)

Figure 223. This Navy officer's dress blue jacket belonged to Lt. (j.g.) William H. Skade CO of PT 143 with RON 8 and XO of PT 625 with RON 43. (Save the PT Boat, Inc. collection)

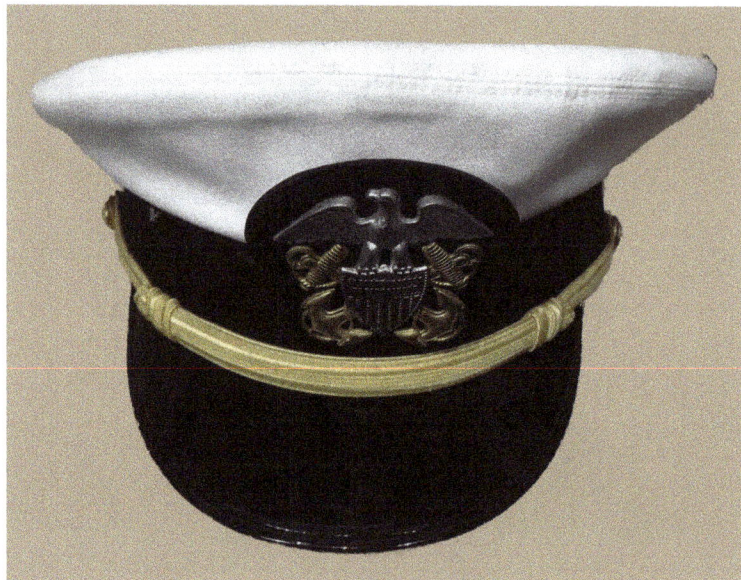

Figure 224. White officer's visor cap belonging to Lt. (j.g.) William H. Skade. (Save the PT Boat, Inc. collection)

Figure 225. A fine example of the N-1 foul weather jacket found on the PT boats. This RON 40 jacket belonged to Dr. Alfred Skinner who served on both PT 591 and PT 595. (Save the PT Boat, Inc. collection)

Figure 226. This is an example of the early blue winter waist-length foul weather jacket. The most popular jacket with collectors today, it featured knit collar, waist, and cuffs and as can be seen in this photo, the cuffs over time were eaten by moths. Rugged as it looks this is a very rare jacket with the MTBSTC Letters on the back. This jacket belonged to Gunner's Mate Robert Sherman who attended the training center in 1944. (PT Boats Inc. collection)

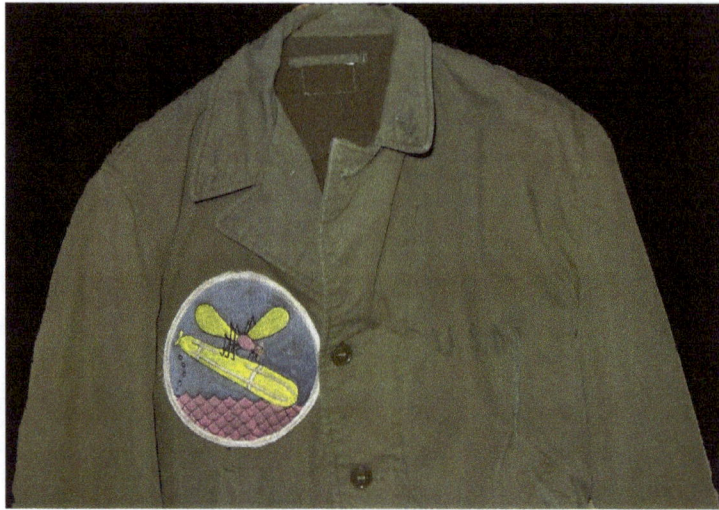

Figure 227. This example of the N-4 Navy green jacket is rare in that it has a MTBSTC patch sewn on. Patches of this type were available in the ship's store at the base. This jacket belonged to Clifford A. Siverling CmoMM RON 4. (Frank J. Andruss Sr. collection)

Figure 228. This example of the N-1 foul weather jacket shows an original RON 39 patch on the breast pocket. On the back of the jacket is stamped MTB RON 39 and 583 as this crewmen was from the 583 boat. Although spotted with some type of spill, it is desirable as a collectible because it has the patch. It belonged to Gunner's Mate C. J. Erickson. (Erickson collection)

Figure 229. Here is a nice N-1 tan jacket that belonged to James "Boats" Newberry who was a Chief Bosun's mate with RON 9 and Chief of Police at the MTBSTC. Newberry founded PT Boats, Inc. as a way to keep in touch with his former shipmates from his squadron. He began a mimeographed Christmas letter to keep his fellow friends informed about squadron news around 1946. (PT Boats Inc. collection)

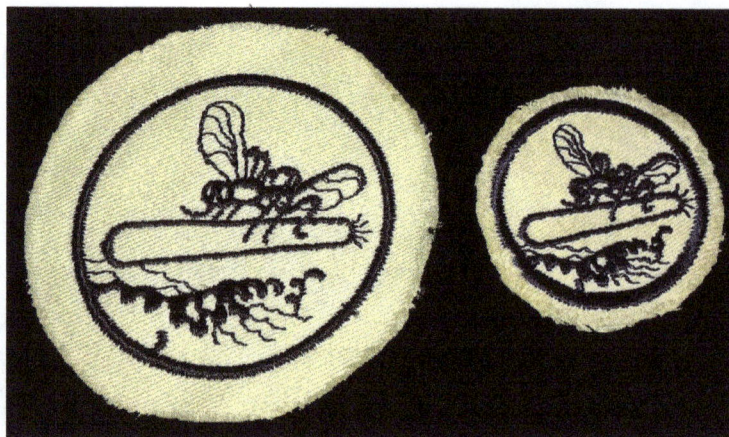

Figure 230. Here are the early style Disney design patches in white, which might be used on the Navy white summer uniform. It should be noted that this design was not accepted by the Navy and wearing one on a uniform could get a sailor into trouble. Most of the time it was tolerated and these patches were usually worn by early squadrons in 1940/41. (Frank J. Andruss Sr. collection)

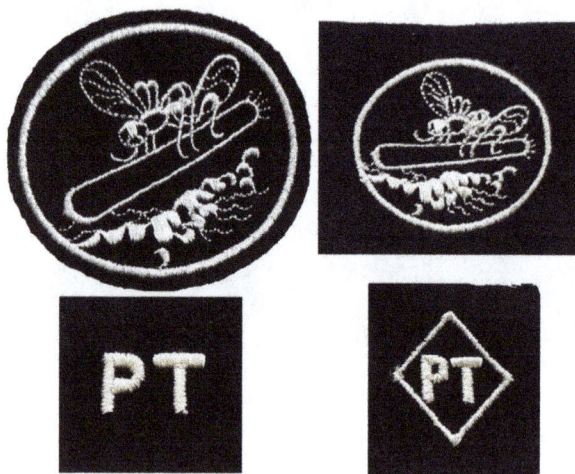

Figure 231. Four examples of PT boat patches. Top row shows the early style patch based on the Disney design--both came in blue and white—but were never formally approved. The bottom row shows the first type that could be officially used on the uniform, with blocked letters PT only. Notice the variation with the letters enclosed in a diamond shape. (Frank J. Andruss Sr. collection)

Figure 232. This is the authorized PT shoulder patch which was worn on the left sleeve, a half inch from the shoulder seam. This design was approved by the Navy in September 1944, and replaced the blocked PT letters. It was circular with rope-design around the edges. Inside we see the letters PT and a torpedo with a line coming off the top and three on the bottom to signify the wake as the torpedo goes through the water. (Frank J. Andruss Sr. collection)

Figure 233. This shoulder patch is what some might call a rare variation in that it is blue. The majority of the accepted shoulder patches were white and black. Some photos exist with this patch on both the blue and white uniforms. (Frank J. Andruss Sr. collection)

Figure 234. Sterling silver PT boat pin. These pins were available at the Elco Naval Division in Bayonne, New Jersey as well as the MTBSTC ship's store, in Rhode Island. (Frank J. Andruss Sr. collection)

Figure 235. Both the gold-plated pin and silver plated pin were available. Here we see on the reverse that these two pins have come from the Elco Naval Division. (Frank J. Andruss Sr. collection)

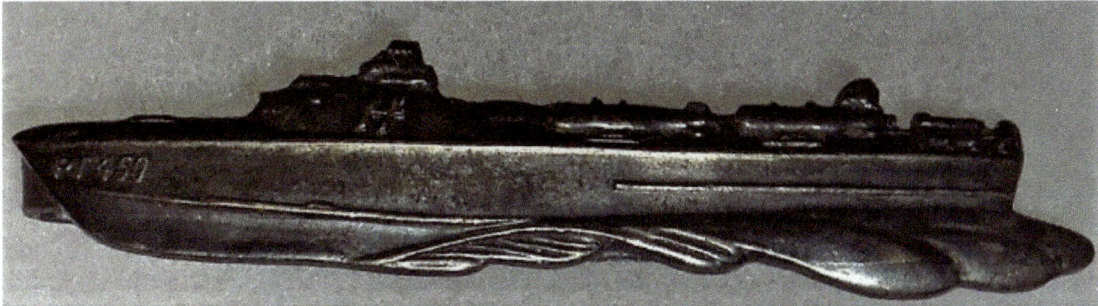

Figure 236. An interesting PT boat pin is this sterling silver pin showing a Higgins PT boat. Stamped on the forward hull is the number 450. This is a tie-clasp pin. (Frank J. Andruss Sr. collection)

Figure 237. Here is another example of the Higgins PT Boat pin. This one is a stick pin design. (Frank J. Andruss Sr. collection)

Figure 238. This photo shows the two different designs of the wave actions for the Elco boat on top and the Higgins boat on the bottom. (Frank J. Andruss Sr. collection)

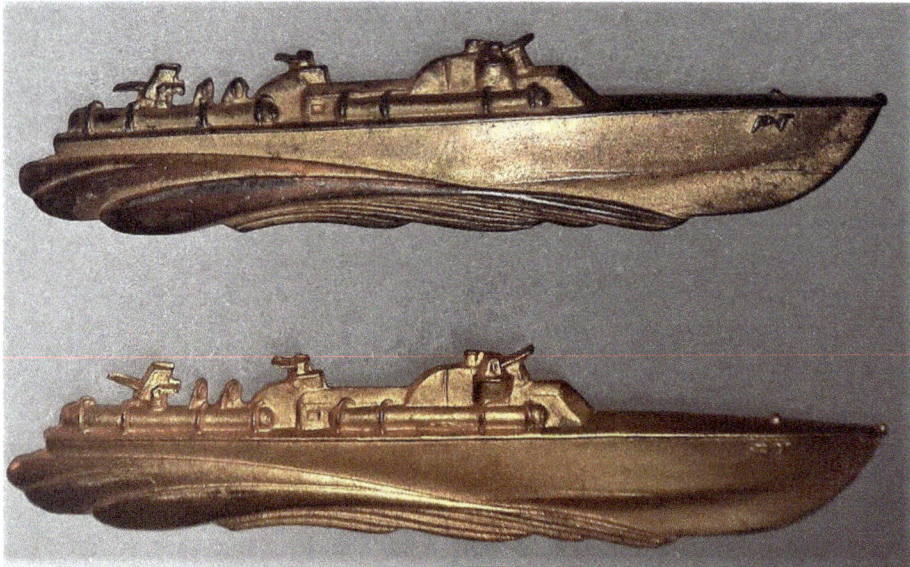

Figure 239. Gold PT boat pins showing another wave design for the boats. (Frank J. Andruss Sr. collection)